ESSAYS in Idleness

Translations from the Asian Classics
Records of Civilization: Sources and Studies

ESSAYS in Idleness

The *TSUREZUREGUSA* of Kenkō

TRANSLATED BY DONALD KEENE

COLUMBIA UNIVERSITY PRESS

NEW YORK

Portions of this work were prepared under a grant from the Carnegie Corporation and a contract with the U. S. Office of Education for the production of texts to be used in undergraduate education. The draft translations so produced have been used in the Columbia College Oriental Humanities program and have subsequently been revised and expanded for publication in the present form.

The illustrations are by Nishikawa Sukenobu (1671–1751).

UNESCO COLLECTION OF REPRESENTATIVE WORKS
Japanese Series
This book
has been accepted
in the Japanese Series
of the Translations Collection
of the United Nations
Educational, Scientific and Cultural Organization
(UNESCO)

*This translation
is dedicated to*
IVAN MORRIS

FOREWORD

Essays in Idleness (*Tsurezuregusa*) is one of the Translations from the Oriental Classics by which the Committee on Oriental Studies has sought to transmit to Western readers representative works of the major Asian traditions in thought and literature. These are works which in our judgment any educated man should have read. Frequently, however, this reading has been denied him by the lack of suitable translations. All too often he has had to choose between excerpts in popular anthologies on the one hand, and on the other heavily annotated translations intended primarily for the specialist, which in many cases are out of date or out of print. Here we offer translations of whole works, based on scholarly studies, but written for the general reader as well as the specialist.

Essays in Idleness has been known to Western readers in the nearly complete translation of Sir George Sansom and in selected excerpts which Professor Keene has included in his *Anthology of Japanese Literature*. Unfortunately the Sansom translation has long been out of print and largely unavailable even in libraries, while the excerpts in the Keene anthology have proven tantalizingly brief to many students of the Oriental Humanities. The fact that the original is itself largely unstructured and fragmentary in form does not make a partial translation any less unsatisfying, while the development of Japanese studies surrounding the essays and their author in the last half-century render a new and complete translation desirable.

The Committee on Oriental Studies is grateful that Professor Keene agreed to perform this service to students, scholars, and the general reader.

WM. THEODORE DE BARY

PREFACE

Essays in Idleness (*Tsurezuregusa*) is a collection of essays ranging in length from a line or two to several pages. It has exercised an influence out of all proportion to its bulk, and would surely be included in any list of the ten most important works of Japanese literature.

So many detailed commentaries have appeared, especially during the past twenty years, that the task of translating the work is far simpler than it was in the past. There are nevertheless many points on which the commentators differ widely. Kenkō's style, though universally praised, is characterized by extreme vagueness. Subjects of sentences are often omitted, and the other clues to the identity of the subject may be inadequate. The translator must make a choice, though he knows it is hardly more than a guess. I have described in my notes some instances where the interpretations most conspicuously vary.

Another problem encountered by every translator is how to render into acceptable English the frequently repeated sentence patterns. Such repetition is not objectionable as far as Japanese style is concerned, but in English it quickly becomes tedious. I have tried to vary the sentences as much as possible, but my object has otherwise been to remain as close to a literal translation as English style will permit. For this reason I have retained, except in a few cases where it would result in unusually cumbrous expressions, Kenkō's practice of referring to people by their titles rather than their names, and his oblique allusions to the writings of the past. I have provided in the notes the necessary factual information, identifying persons mentioned and so on, but in general the notes are intended for the specialist and are not necessary for ready understanding of the text.

Of the half dozen or so earlier translations of the work into English or German, the one published by G. B. Sansom in 1911 under the title *The Tsuredzure Gusa of Yoshida no Kaneyoshi* is the most distinguished. I have known it for years, and undoubtedly many phrases in my translation are derived from Sansom's text. The present version, however, has benefited by scholarship in Japan during the past half century, and I have tried to impart to the English a more modern flavor than Sansom's. The translation is complete. There are few textual variants of consequence in *Essays in Idleness,* but when faced by a discrepancy I have chosen to follow the text edited by Nishio Minoru in the Nihon Koten Bungaku Taikei series. Other works consulted are listed in the Bibliography.

In translating titles, the names of buildings, and the like, I have generally been guided by the choices of Robert K. Reischauer in *Early Japanese History.* The material given in my notes is derived from three centuries of Japanese scholarship, but much was taken directly from Tanabe Tsukasa, *Tsurezuregusa Shochū Shūsei* (Compendium of various commentaries on *Tsurezuregusa*). When a person mentioned in the text has not yet been identified, despite the researches of generations of Japanese scholars, I have usually passed over the person in silence rather than recount the fruitless attempts to discover his identity. Fortunately, there can hardly be a work of literature which has been better served by the savants.

Karuizawa–New York, 1965–66   DONALD KEENE

[x]

CONTENTS

INTRODUCTION

Essays in Idleness (*Tsurezuregusa*) seems to have been written between 1330 and 1332. This was not a propitious time for a work of reflection and comment. In 1331 Go-Daigo, the emperor, staged a revolt against the actual rulers of Japan, the Hōjō family, and in the following year, after his defeat, was exiled to the lonely Oki islands. In the meantime the Hōjō family set up another prince as emperor. In 1333 Go-Daigo returned from exile and his supporters succeeded in overthrowing the Hōjō rule, which had lasted almost a century and a half. These events and the many incidents that presaged them created great anxiety among the educated classes, but they hardly ruffle the surface of *Essays in Idleness*. The author tells us in the first sentence that he wrote by way of diversion from boredom, jotting down whatever came into his head. *Essays in Idleness* is an expression neither of sorrow over troubled times, nor of joy over the temporary successes of one or another party; it is instead a work of timeless relevance, a splendid example of Japanese meditative style.

The author is generally known by his name as a Buddhist priest, Kenkō, but sometimes also by his lay name of Urabe no Kaneyoshi or by the name Yoshida no Kaneyoshi, derived from his long residence at Yoshida in Kyoto. We cannot be sure when he was born or died, but most scholars believe that he lived from 1283 to 1350. His family were hereditary Shintō priests of modest rank, but the youthful

Kenkō was able, thanks to his abilities as a poet, to secure a place at the court. Kenkō's poetry is likely to strike us as conservative or even dull, but these qualities were precisely those most esteemed by the reigning school of poetry, which frowned on innovation and originality as betrayals of tradition.

Kenkō took Buddhist orders in 1324, after the death of the Retired Emperor Go-Uda, whom he had served. Many theories have been put forward to explain Kenkō's reasons for "leaving the world," but nothing in his writings suggests that it was an act of despair. Buddhist thought figures prominently in the pages of *Essays in Idleness,* but Kenkō bears little resemblance to the hermit-priests whose writings dominate medieval Japan. Kenkō remained in the city, as familiar with worldly gossip as with pious reflections on the vanity of this world, seemingly unconcerned with theological disputes. Specific Buddhist doctrines occasionally figure in his pages, but the most important Buddhist influences are those underlying his views of the nature of the world. The impermanence of all things; the endless cycle of birth, growth, sickness, and death, followed again by birth; the vanity of worldly achievements and possessions are typical Buddhist beliefs expressed in *Essays in Idleness* with a freshness that compels admiration.

Little is known about the manner of composition of *Essays in Idleness.* For many years the account by Sanjōnishi Saneeda (1511–79) was accepted. This stated that Kenkō did not himself edit the 243 chapters comprising the work; instead, Kenkō wrote his thoughts on scraps of paper which he pasted to the walls of his cottage. The poet and general Imagawa Ryōshun, learning of this unusual wallpaper, carefully removed the many scraps, combined them with some essays in the possession of Kenkō's former servant, and arranged them in the present order. Modern critics generally reject this account, doubting that anyone other than Kenkō himself could have put together the fragments so skillfully. No doubt, however, some basis existed for the association of Ryōshun's name with the manuscript. The oldest surviving text of *Essays in Idleness,* dated 1431, is in the hand of Shōtetsu, a disciple of Ryōshun. The title too seems to date from that time, but the present division of the text into a preface and 243 numbered episodes can be traced back only to the seventeenth century.

Essays in Idleness apparently was unknown to the public during Kenkō's lifetime. His reputation was that of a poet, though not one of the first magnitude. His indifference to politics, apparent in the *Essays,* is suggested also by his ready shift of allegiance to the new régime when the Emperor Go-Daigo returned in triumph to Kyoto in 1333, and then to the régime of the Ashikaga shoguns in 1336, when Go-Daigo was again driven into exile. Kenkō, we know, took part in the regular tri-monthly poetry gatherings at the palace, begun in 1346. Nijō Yoshimoto (1320–88), the leading poet of his day, said of Kenkō that "people considered him inferior to others of this company, but his poems were widely quoted." Kenkō's reputation as a poet was nevertheless sufficiently great for him to be referred to as one of the "four heavenly kings" of poetry.

In his last years Kenkō lived at Kanshin-in, a temple in the Yoshida area of Kyoto, well known as a poet and an expert on old traditions. He associated with the new military overlords of Japan, notably with Kō no Moronao (d. 1351), a violent warrior who desired the trappings of a cultured man. It is hard to imagine Kenkō taking on such a man as his pupil, but perhaps his financial situation made this necessary.

The Work

Comparisons have frequently been made between *Essays in Idleness* and *The Pillow Book* of Sei Shōnagon, a collection of anecdotes and observations written about the year 1000. Both works belong to the random mode of composition known as *zuihitsu* (follow the brush) in Japanese. This form—or lack of form—was most congenial to Japanese writers, who turned to it perhaps because it was less "dishonest" than creating fiction. The formlessness of the *zuihitsu* did not impede enjoyment by readers; indeed, they took pleasure not only in moving from one to another of the great variety of subjects treated but in tracing subtle links joining the successive episodes. *The Pillow Book* is the first masterpiece of *zuihitsu,* and Kenkō knew it well, but the differences between it and *Essays in Idleness* are more striking than the resemblances, even though both afford the pleasures of the *zuihitsu* style. Some differences arise simply because Sei Shōnagon was a fashionable court lady and Kenkō a Buddhist priest. Sei Shōnagon is often cruelly witty and delights in exposing the ridiculous; Kenkō has humor, but it is not so much the flashing repartee that might be exchanged between men and women at the court as the amusing anecdotes old cronies might relate. Her perceptions are sharp if not always profound; his are generally linked with some statement of Buddhist truths.

One important strain in *Essays in Idleness,* entirely absent from *The Pillow Book,* is the conviction that the world is steadily growing worse. For Sei Shōnagon, writing in an age which scorned the crudities of the past, being up to date was more important than knowing about precedent, but for Kenkō the least important tradition of the past was a precious survival that must be preserved, regardless of its merits. Kenkō was impressed by the Abbess Genki who remembered from childhood that the "bell-shaped windows in the Kan'in Palace were rounder and without frames." What did it matter, we may wonder, if the windows in the new palace were slightly different in shape? But for Kenkō a window-shape at variance with the old traditions reflected the degeneracy of the age; it was certainly not a sign of progress. Kenkō was dismayed that "nobody is left who knows the proper manner of hanging a quiver before the house of a man in disgrace with His Majesty," and even regretted that no one knew any longer the proper shape of a torture rack nor the manner of attaching a criminal.

Kenkō's clinging to traditions, his reluctance to accept change reveal an attachment to this world unbecoming a true monk. Kenkō did not choose to live on a lonely mountainside; precedent and custom were elements of stability that enabled him to create a refuge for himself within society. He frequently tells us how much he appreciates the pleasures of solitude, but only five of his 243 episodes are devoted to descriptions of nature, the conventional solace of the hermit. He displays on the other hand an unbounded interest in the old usages of the court surprising in one who, having renounced the world to become a priest, should have been indifferent to mundane traditions.

Despite the overt attention given to Buddhism in certain episodes, and the unspoken acceptance of many Buddhist beliefs, the most memorable parts of *Essays in Idleness* are devoted to secular themes, particularly the nature of beauty.

Kenkō put forward the most peculiarly Japanese of aesthetic principles: beauty is indissolubly bound to its perishability. He wrote, "If man were never to fade away like the dews of Adashino, never to vanish like the smoke over Toribeyama, but lingered on forever in this world, how things would lose their power to move us! The most precious thing in life is its uncertainty." Undoubtedly Buddhist influence is present in this statement, but Buddhists rarely saw the impermanence of things as desirable or pleasant. Nor do Kenkō's views accord with those commonly found in the West from the days of the Greeks, that uncertainty is the source of grief. Yet the Japanese appreciation of impermanence surely lies behind their love for the cherry blossoms or their preference for building houses of perishable wood and paper rather than of stone. The falling of the cherry blossoms is always regretted, but their very brevity gives them beauty. By a curious paradox, wooden temples and statues of a thousand years ago survive in Japan, having seemingly acquired permanence despite their materials, but the attempt was never consciously made to achieve the deathlessness of marble or to defy the ravages of time. Whatever has survived has aged, and the faded quality, the reminder of impermanence despite long survival, has been especially prized. Kenkō quoted with approbation the poet Ton'a who said, "It is only after the silk wrapper has frayed at top and bottom, and the mother-of-pearl has fallen from the roller, that a scroll looks beautiful." Lafcadio Hearn once termed the appreciation of perishability "the genius of Japanese civilization."

Kenkō's pleasure in impermanence was joined to a fondness for the irregular and the incomplete. He said, "In everything, no matter what it may be, uniformity is undesirable. Leaving something incomplete makes it interesting, and gives one the feeling that there is room for growth." Or again, "It is typical of the unintelligent man to insist on assembling complete sets of everything. Imperfect sets are better." Undoubtedly most people in Kenkō's day, no less than in our own, preferred complete sets and objects of art in flawless condition, but the connoisseur, the true admirer of beauty, desires more than banal perfection. The most valued bowls for the tea ceremony are irregularly shaped, and some have gold patches here and there accentuating (rather than concealing) damage suffered at the hands of long-ago owners. Asymmetry and irregularity allow the possibility of growth, but perfection chokes the imagination.

Another aspect of Kenkō's advocacy of the imperfect is his belief in the importance of beginnings and ends. "Are we to look at cherry blossoms only in full bloom, the moon only when it is cloudless? To long for the moon while looking on the rain, to lower the blinds and be unaware of the passing of the spring—these are even more deeply moving. Branches about to blossom or gardens strewn with faded flowers are worthier of our admiration." The statement is by no means obvious. Even in Japan a pleasure in the imperfect has not often compelled people to look at cherry blossoms still in the bud or else scattered, and in the West the climactic moment has been emphasized, whether of the rose in full glory or of the soprano when she reaches high C. "In all things," Kenkō continues, "it is the beginnings and ends that are interesting." Suggestion, a characteristic feature of all forms of Japanese art, is best served by the imperfect, whether that of the beginning (with its promise) or that of the end (with its evocations of the past). The hoped-for love affair or regrets over parting are often treated in Japanese poetry, but hardly a poem mentions accomplished love. We can add nothing with our imagination to the full moon nor to blossoms at their peak; they are complete.

Irregularity and incompleteness go well with simplicity, which also suggests more than it states. Kenkō wrote, "A house which multitudes of workmen have polished with every care, where strange and rare Chinese and Japanese furnishings are displayed, and even the grasses and trees of the garden have been trained unnaturally, is ugly to look at and most depressing." It is easy for us to assent to this opinion, but the richly appointed house has usually been considered in the West most beautiful and agreeable to live in. In Japan too the polychrome carvings of the Tokugawa Mausoleum at Nikkō remind one that simplicity has not always been considered the mark of good taste. Simplicity, which allows the mind freedom to imagine, to create, did not appeal to nineteenth-century observers of Japanese architecture, who contrasted its insignificance with the grandeur of European masterpieces, but today our tastes are better attuned to the understatement advocated by Kenkō.

Understatement was a merit for Kenkō not only in architecture but in civilized behavior. *Essays in Idleness* is in one sense a manual of gentlemanly conduct. "A man should avoid displaying deep familiarity with any subject. Can one imagine a well-bred man talking with the airs of a know-it-all, even about a matter with which he is in fact familiar? . . . It is impressive when a man is always slow to speak, even on subjects he knows thoroughly, and does not speak at all unless questioned." Kenkō's gentleman may remind us of Castiglione's courtier: "I have found it quite a universal rule which in this matter seems to me valid above all others, and in all human affairs whether in word or deed: and that is to avoid affectation in every way possible as though it were some very rough and dangerous reef; and to practice in all things a certain nonchalance, so as to conceal all art and make whatever is done or said appear to be without effort and almost without any thought about it."

Kenkō constantly compared his ideal gentleman with the insensitive, boorish people who made up most of society. "The man of breeding never appears to abandon himself completely to his pleasures; even his manner of enjoyment is detached. It is the rustic boors who take all their pleasures grossly." Restraint in behavior, the equivalent of understatement in artistic expression, marked the gentleman. "When the well-bred man tells a story he addresses himself to one person, even if many people are present, though the others too listen, naturally. But the ill-bred man flings out his words into the crowd, addressing himself to no one in particular, and describes what happened so graphically that everyone bursts into boisterous laughter. You can judge a person's breeding by whether he is quite impassive even when he tells an amusing story or laughs a great deal even when relating a matter of no interest."

Kenkō's views on aesthetics or on gentlemanly behavior make up a coherent argument, but on other matters we find contradictions. He expresses, for example, admiration for those who remain childless, but declares also that a man without children cannot appreciate the beauty of things. Again, within the same section he describes the horrors of drink but also the pleasure of drinking and even of forcing someone against his will to drink. Some contradictions may be the result of the casual manner of composition, random thoughts jotted down over a period of time, but in any case, Kenkō is a suggestive rather than a systematic thinker.

Essays in Idleness, despite such inconsistencies and despite a number of uninteresting sections on forgotten ceremonials and usages, is an attractive and moving work. In Japan it has ranked as a classic ever since the seventeenth century when detailed commentaries began to appear and the work was adopted as a basic element in educating the young. *Essays in Idleness* was taken as a model of Japanese prose. No doubt many of the thoughts contained in its pages were in this manner absorbed by young Japanese. It remains today an essential part of the school curriculum; over one hundred commentated editions have been published since 1945 alone, and students can be sure that university entrance examinations will have at least one question on *Essays in Idleness.*

The influence of *Essays in Idleness* has extended in many directions. Allusions to Kenkō's writings are found in plays, novels, and poetry, and his opinions have been adopted by many persons ignorant of the source. The factory worker who goes to see the cherry blossoms may not be aware that the special importance of these blossoms (as opposed to plum or peach blossoms) derives from long aesthetic traditions, but he would understand at once if told that cherry blossoms are prized because so short-lived. Kenkō may not have been the first to discover this principle, but he gives it a most persuasive statement.

Essays in Idleness is a central work in the development of Japanese taste. Though Kenkō's argumentation is not sustained and often consists merely in a brief statement of perceptions, he succeeded in defining with great sensitivity aesthetic preferences that have been true of Japan ever since.

ESSAYS in Idleness

What a strange, demented feeling it gives me when I realize I have spent whole days before this inkstone, with nothing better to do,[1] jotting down at random whatever nonsensical thoughts have entered my head.

1. *Tsurezure naru mama ni*, translated here as "with nothing better to do," opens the introductory section and gives rise to the title, *Tsurezuregusa*.

I

It is enough, it would seem, to have been born into this world for a man to desire many things. The position of the emperor, of course, is far too exalted for our aspirations. Even the remote descendants of the imperial line[1] are sacred, for they are not of the seed of man. Ordinary nobles[2] of a rank that entitles them to retainers—let alone those who stand in the solitary grandeur of the chancellor—appear most impressive, and even their children and grandchildren, though their fortunes may decline, still possess a distinctive elegance. Persons of lower rank, fortunate enough to achieve some success in keeping with their station, are apt to wear looks of self-satisfaction and no doubt consider themselves most important, but actually they are quite insignificant.

No one is less to be envied than a priest. Sei Shōnagon[3] wrote of priests that they seemed to outsiders "like sticks of wood," an apt description. The clerics impress nobody, even when they flaunt their authority and their importance is loudly proclaimed. It is easy to see why the holy man Sōga[4] should have said that worldly fame is unseemly in priests, and that those who seek it violate the teachings of Buddha. A true hermit might, in fact, seem more admirable.

It is desirable that a man's face and figure be of excelling beauty. I could sit forever with a man, provided that what he said did not grate on my ears, that he had charm, and that he did not talk very much. What an unpleasant experience it is when someone you have supposed to be quite distinguished reveals his true, inferior nature. A man's social position and looks are likely to be determined at birth, but why should not a man's mind go from wisdom to greater wisdom if it is so disposed? What a shame it is when men of excellent appearance and character prove hopelessly inept in social encounters with their inferiors in both position and appearance, solely because they are badly educated.

A familiarity with orthodox scholarship,[5] the ability to compose poetry and prose in Chinese, a knowledge of Japanese poetry and music are all desirable, and if a man can serve as a model to others in matters of precedent and court ceremony, he is truly impressive. The mark of an excellent man is that he writes easily in an acceptable hand, sings agreeably and in tune, and, though appearing reluctant to accept when wine is pressed on him, is not a teetotaler.

1. *Take no sonō no sueha* means literally "last leaves of the bamboo garden," a reference to the park built by King Hsiao of Liang; it came to mean descendants of a royal house.
2. *Tadabito* were nobles not of sufficient rank to be eligible for the posts of regent or chancellor.
3. Sei Shōnagon, the author of *The Pillow Book*, lived from about 965 to about 1010. Her work much influenced Kenkō.
4. Sōga (917–1003), a high ranking priest of the Tendai sect, spent his last years in a lonely retreat. His name is sometimes read Zōga.
5. Scholarship in the Confucian sense—learning useful in governing a country or of intrinsic moral value.

2

The man who forgets the wise principles of the reigns of the ancient emperors; who gives no thought to the grievances of the people or the harm done the country; who strives for the utmost luxury in everything, imagining this is the sign of magnificence; who acts as if the world were too small for him seems deplorably wanting in intelligence. You will find in Lord Kujō's Testament[1] the instruction, "Make do with whatever you have, from your court costume down to your horses and carriages. Do not strive for elegance." Again, you will find among the writings of the Retired Emperor Juntoku[2] on court ceremonial, "The clothes worn by the emperor should be simple and unassuming."

1. Kujō-dono was an appellation of Fujiwara no Morosuke (908–960). His Testament (or Admonitions) is translated in G. B. Sansom, *A History of Japan to 1334*, pp. 180–83.
2. The Emperor Juntoku (1197–1242) wrote *Kimpishō*, a study of court precedents and usages, between 1218 and 1221. Kenkō's quotation is approximate.

3

A man may excel at everything else, but if he has no taste for lovemaking, one feels something terribly inadequate about him, as if he were a valuable winecup without a bottom. What a charming figure is the lover, his clothes drenched with dew or frost, wandering about aimlessly, so fearful of his parents' reproaches or people's gossip that he has not a moment's peace of mind, frantically resorting to one unsuccessful stratagem after another; and for all that, most often sleeping alone, though never soundly. But it is best that a

man not be given over completely to fleshly pleasures, and
that women not consider him an easy conquest.

4

It is admirable when a man keeps his thoughts constantly on
the future life and is not remiss in his devotions to the Way
of the Buddha.

5

It is better for a man sunken in grief over misfortunes to
shut his gate and live in seclusion, so quietly, awaiting nothing, that people cannot tell whether or not he is at home,
rather than that he hastily decide to shave his head and become a priest. Akimoto,[1] the middle counselor, once spoke
of wishing "to see the moon of exile, though guilty of no
crime." It is easy to imagine why he felt so.[2]

1. Minamoto no Akimoto (1000–47) abandoned a promising career as an
official to take Buddhist orders in 1036, after the death of the Emperor
Go-Ichijō.
2. Many Japanese commentators express bewilderment over Akimoto's
wish; presumably, he desired to enter into the emotions of famous poets
who had seen the moon in exile. It is hard to believe he actually longed
to be exiled.

6

Even members of the nobility, let alone persons of no consequence, would do well not to have children. Prince Kanea-

kira, Fujiwara no Koremichi, and Minamoto no Arihito[1] all desired that their line end with themselves. Fujiwara no Yoshifusa,[2] according to the account in *Ōkagami*,[3] was of the same opinion. He wrote, "You would best not have descendants. How unfortunate it would be if they proved inferior to yourself!" They say that when Prince Shōtoku[4] had a tomb built for himself before his death, he ordered the workmen to "cut here, trim there—I wish for no descendants."

1. I have called these men by name, but the text lists them by office. Kaneakira (914–87) was the son of the Emperor Daigo. Fujiwara no Koremichi (1093–1165) actually had three children. Minamoto no Arihito (1103–47) was a grandson of the Emperor Sanjō.
2. Fujiwara no Yoshifusa (804–72) rose to be prime minister. He had one child, a daughter.
3. *Ōkagami* (Great Mirror) is a historical romance covering the period 850 to 1025, probably written late in the eleventh century. Kenkō refers to the work by an alternative title, *Yotsugi no Okina no Monogatari*. The quotation is not found in any extant version.
4. Prince Shōtoku (573–621), according to the biography compiled in 917, ordered his tomb to be built on a humble scale so that his posterity would die out. By the same reasoning, a splendid tomb would have caused them to prosper.

7

If man were never to fade away like the dews of Adashino,[1] never to vanish like the smoke over Toribeyama,[2] but lingered on forever in the world, how things would lose their power to move us![3] The most precious thing in life is its uncertainty. Consider living creatures—none lives so long as man. The May fly waits not for the evening, the summer cicada knows neither spring nor autumn. What a wonderfully unhurried feeling it is to live even a single year in perfect serenity! If that is not enough for you, you might live a thousand years and still feel it was but a single night's dream. We cannot live forever in this world; why should we wait for ugliness to overtake us? The longer man lives, the more shame he endures. To die, at the latest, before one reaches forty, is the least unattractive. Once a man passes that age, he desires (with no sense of shame over his appearance) to mingle in the company of others. In his sunset years he dotes on his grandchildren, and prays for long life so that he may see them prosper. His preoccupation with worldly desires grows ever deeper, and gradually he loses all sensitivity to the beauty of things, a lamentable state of affairs.

1. Adashino was the name of a graveyard, apparently situated northwest of Kyoto. The word *adashi* (impermanent), contained in the place name, accounted for the frequent use of Adashino in poetry as a symbol of impermanence. The dew is also often used with that meaning.
2. Toribeyama is still the chief graveyard of Kyoto. Mention of smoke suggests that bodies were cremated there.
3. The well-known expression *mono no aware* is here translated as "the power of things to move us." It has also been translated as "the pity of things," a more literal meaning.

8

Nothing leads a man astray so easily as sexual desire. What a foolish thing a man's heart is! Though we realize, for example, that fragrances are short-lived and the scent burnt into clothes[1] lingers but briefly, how our hearts always leap when we catch a whiff of an exquisite perfume! The holy man of Kume[2] lost his magic powers after noticing the whiteness of the legs of a girl who was washing clothes; this was quite understandable, considering that the glowing plumpness of her arms, legs, and flesh owed nothing to artifice.

1. Incense was burnt in a room until clothes hanging there were impermeated with scent. The meaning here is that, while we know that scents are artificial and not part of the woman, yet they stir us all the same.
2. The holy man of Kume figures in tales dating back to the tenth century. His magic power was an ability to fly through the air.

9

Beautiful hair, of all things in a woman, is most likely to catch a man's eye. Her character and temperament may be guessed from the first words she utters, even if she is hidden behind a screen. When a woman somehow—perhaps unintentionally—has captured a man's heart she is generally unable to sleep peacefully. She will not hesitate to subject herself to hardships, and will even endure cheerfully what she would normally find intolerable, all because love means so much to her.

The love of men and women is truly a deep-seated passion with distant roots. The senses give rise to many desires, but it should be possible to shun them all. Only one, infatuation, is impossible to control; old or young, wise or foolish, in this respect all seem identical. That is why they say that even a great elephant can be fastened securely with a rope plaited from the strands of a woman's hair,[1] and that a flute made from a sandal a woman has worn will infallibly summon the autumn deer.[2] We must guard against this delusion of the senses, which is to be dreaded and avoided.

1. The expression is of Buddhist origin, but the source is not known.
2. This claim for a woman's *geta* is not found elsewhere.

A house, I know, is but a temporary abode, but how delightful it is to find one that has harmonious proportions and a
pleasant atmosphere. One feels somehow that even moonlight, when it shines into the quiet domicile of a person of
taste, is more affecting than elsewhere. A house, though it
may not be in the current fashion or elaborately decorated,
will appeal to us by its unassuming beauty—a grove of trees
with an indefinably ancient look; a garden where plants,
growing of their own accord, have a special charm; a verandah and an open-work wooden fence of interesting construction; and a few personal effects left carelessly lying about, giving the place an air of having been lived in. A house which
multitudes of workmen have polished with every care, where
strange and rare Chinese and Japanese furnishings are displayed, and even the grasses and trees of the garden have
been trained unnaturally, is ugly to look at and most depressing. How could anyone live for long in such a place? The
most casual glance will suggest how likely such a house is.
to turn in a moment to smoke.

A man's character, as a rule, may be known from the place
where he lives. The Gotokudaiji minister[1] stretched a rope
across his roof to keep the kites from roosting. Saigyō,[2] seeing the rope, asked, "Why should it bother him if kites perch
there? That shows you the kind of man this prince is." I have
heard that Saigyō never visited him again. I remembered this
story not long ago when I noticed a rope stretched over the
roof of the Kosaka palace,[3] where Prince Ayanokōji[4] lives.
Someone told me that, as a matter of fact, it distressed the
prince to see how crows clustering on the roof would swoop
down to seize frogs in the pond. The story impressed me,

and made me wonder if Sanesada may not also have had some such reason.

1. Fujiwara no Sanesada (1139–91), a poet.
2. Saigyō (1118–90), one of the greatest Japanese poets.
3. Another name for the Tendai temple Myōhō-in. Some scholars read the name as Osaka.
4. The prince was a son of the Emperor Kameyama (1249–1305), and was also known by his Buddhist name, Shōe. An imperial prince still resides at Myōhō-in.

I I

About the tenth month I had the occasion to visit a village beyond the place called Kurusuno.[1] I made my way far down a moss-covered path until I reached a lonely-looking hut. Not a sound could be heard, except for the dripping of a water pipe buried in fallen leaves. Sprays of chrysanthemum and red maple leaves had been carelessly arranged on the holy-water shelf. Evidently somebody was living here. Moved, I was thinking, "One can live even in such a place," when I noticed in the garden beyond a great tangerine tree, its branches bent with fruit, that had been enclosed by a forbidding fence. Rather disillusioned, I thought now, "If only the tree had not been there!"

1. A village east of Kyoto.

I 2

How delightful it would be to converse intimately with someone of the same mind, sharing with him the pleasures of uninhibited conversation on the amusing and foolish things of this world, but such friends are hard to find. If you must take care that your opinions do not differ in the least from those of the person with whom you are talking, you might just as well be alone. You might suppose that a man who listens in general agreement to what the other person is saying, but differs on minor points—who may contest an opinion, saying, "How can I possibly agree?" or argue, "It's precisely because of *this* that *that* is the case"—would be a great comfort when you were bored, but as a matter of fact, if ever anything is said which might require a word of apology[1]—of course, even when conversing with people who are not of the same mind, differences over the usual insignificant gossip do not matter—one realizes sadly what a great distance separates this man from the true friends of one's heart.

1. This passage is ambiguous. The words *sukoshi kakotsu kata mo* have also been interpreted as meaning "if when making complaints about the world one is not in accord . . ." or "if ever there is anything on which both parties do not agree."

13

The pleasantest of all diversions is to sit alone under the lamp, a book spread out before you, and to make friends with people of a distant past you have never known. The books I would choose are the moving volumes of *Wen Hsüan*,[1] the collected works of Po Chü-i, the sayings of Lao Tzu, and the chapters of Chuang Tzu. Among works by scholars of this country, those written long ago are often quite interesting.

1. A collection of poetry compiled by Prince Chao Ming of Liang (501–31). It was known as *Monzen* in Japan and exercised great influence. The phrase may be interpreted as meaning Kenkō would read *Wen Hsüan*, which consisted of moving volumes, or that he would read only the moving sections of *Wen Hsüan*.

14

There is charm too in the *waka*.[1] The toil of the humblest peasant or woodcutter sounds delightful when described in a *waka,* and even the ferocious boar becomes gentle when the poets speak of "the couch of the sleeping boar."

Poems of recent times occasionally seem to contain an aptly turned line or two, but I wonder why one never senses in them as in the old poetry overtones going beyond the words. Tsurayuki's poem beginning, "Although it is not twisted together of threads" has the reputation of being among the dregs of the poetry in the *Kokinshū*,[2] but I doubt that any poet today could display such mastery of style. The poems of that age are characterized by similar form and diction; I cannot understand why this particular poem should have acquired such a bad reputation. It is quoted in *The Tale of Genji* with the second line given as *mono to wa nashi ni*.[3] The poem in the *Shinkokinshū*[4] ending, "Even the pines, that remain unaffected, are lonely on the peak," has also been called a failure, and indeed the form seems somewhat irregular. However, even this poem was adjudged to be quite superior when it was submitted to a poetry competition, and in later times it especially touched an emperor, as we know from Ienaga's[5] diary.

Some hold that the way of poetry alone remains unchanged since ancient times, but I wonder how true that is. The same words and subjects that might still be employed today meant something quite different when employed by the poets of ancient times. Their poems are simple and unaffected, and the lovely purity of the form creates a powerful impression.

The language of the ballads[6] in *Ryōjin Hishō* is also often marked by intensity of feeling. Why is it that even the most

つれづれなるままに、ひぐらし、硯にむかひて、心にうつりゆくよしなし事を、そこはかとなく書きつくれば、あやしうこそものぐるほしけれ

"The pleasantest of all diversions is to sit alone under the lamp, a book spread out before you . . ."

careless utterance of the men of former days should sound so splendid?

1. The classic Japanese verse form, in five lines of 5, 7, 5, 7, 7 syllables.
2. *Kokinshū* (Collection of ancient and modern poetry) was compiled in 905 by Ki no Tsurayuki. The poem runs in translation, "Although it is not twisted together of threads, how forlorn the road on which we part seems!" The poem devolves on a play on words between *hosoi* (slender), an adjective used of threads, and *kokorobosoi* (forlorn), used of the poet's feelings. The road is not twisted together of threads—if it were, the poet could see why it would grow thinner when unraveled—but his feelings are as forlorn as towards something fragile as threads. The poem is based on a conceit, and is likely to strike a modern reader as indeed belonging to the dregs of *Kokinshū*.
3. The second line in *Kokinshū* is *mono naranaku ni,* but the meaning is similar.
4. *Shinkokinshū* (New collection of ancient and modern poetry) was compiled in 1206. The poem referred to is by Hafuribe Narishige and runs, "Winter has come; the leaves have all fallen and the mountains are bare. Even the pines that remain unaffected are lonely on the peak."
5. Minamoto Ienaga (1170–1234) was for a time second in command of the *Wakadokoro,* or Poetry Office.
6. The ballads (*eikyoku*) included *kagurauta, saibara, imayō,* and other types of verse not in the *waka* form. *Ryōjin Hishō* is an anthology of ballads, compiled by the Emperor Go-Shirakawa.

15

It wakes you up to take a journey for a while, wherever it may be. As you walk around the place, looking here and there at rustic scenes and mountain villages, everything seems most unfamiliar. And how amusing it is the way people snatch the first opportunity to send a letter back to the capital: "When you get the chance, don't forget to do this, don't forget to do that." In such a place you really notice everything. Anything good—even the possessions you have brought

along with you—seems better, and anyone you meet with
artistic talent or handsome features seems more impressive
than he usually would. It is delightful also to go into retreat
at some temple or shrine, unknown to anyone.

16

Kagura[1] is charming and full of interest. In general, I enjoy
the sound of the flute and reed pipe when played as the accompaniment for *kagura*,[2] but for everyday listening, I prefer
the *biwa* and the *wagon*.[3]

1. *Kagura* consists of dances performed to a text sung by a chorus and accompanied by various instruments. It is most often performed at Shinto
   shrines, but Kenkō refers here to *kagura* at the palace.
2. The literal meaning is, "In general, among the sounds of instruments
   (there are) flute and reed pipe. What I would like to hear all the time
   are *biwa* and *wagon*." This seems to suggest that the flute and reed pipe
   (*hichiriki*) are desirable only as an accompaniment for *kagura*.
3. The *biwa* is a stringed instrument resembling the lute. The *wagon* is a
   variety of zither.

17

When you go into retreat at a mountain temple and serve the
Buddha, you are never at a loss how to spend your time, and
you feel as though the impurities in your heart are being
cleansed away.

18

It is excellent for a man to be simple in his tastes, to avoid
extravagance, to own no possessions, to entertain no craving

for worldly success. It has been true since ancient days that wise men are rarely rich. In China there was once a man called Hsü Yu[1] who owned not a single possession. Someone, seeing him use his hands to scoop up water for drinking, presented him with what is known as a "sounding gourd." [2] For a time Hsü Yu hung it on the branch of a tree, but it rattled when the wind blew. "How noisy!" he said, and threw it away. Hsü Yu went back to drinking water scooped up in his hands. What a clean detachment must have been in his heart!

Sun Ch'en[3] slept without a quilt during the winter months. All he had was a bundle of straw that he slept on at night and put away in the morning. The Chinese considered these men so notable that they recorded their biographies for the sake of later generations. People in our country would not even think it worth mentioning them.[4]

1. A famous hermit of Chinese legend. When the Emperor Yao indicated his intention of abdicating in Hsü Yu's favor, the latter washed his ears, feeling they had been defiled by this mundane proposal. The story of throwing away the gourd derives from *Meng Ch'iu* by Li Han, a collection of anecdotes about famous men. It was transmitted to Japan by 1204 when Minamoto no Mitsuyuki included it in *Mōkyū Waka,* a selection from *Meng Ch'iu* translated into Japanese with *waka* appended. Kenkō's text follows *Mōkyū Waka.*
2. *Narihisago* was a common word for gourd, but the first part, *nari,* suggests "sounding." Gourds were used as drinking vessels.
3. The story of Sun Ch'en is found in *Meng Ch'iu* and in *Mōkyū Waka.*
4. That is, Japanese are so partial to display that they would ignore such examples of simplicity.

19

The changing of the seasons is deeply moving in its every manifestation. People seem to agree that autumn is the best

season to appreciate the beauty of things. That may well be true, but the sights of spring are even more exhilarating. The cries of the birds gradually take on a peculiarly springlike quality, and in the gentle sunlight the bushes begin to sprout along the fences. Then, as spring deepens, mists spread over the landscape and the cherry blossoms seem ready to open, only for steady rains and winds to cause them to scatter precipitously. The heart is subject to incessant pangs of emotion as the young leaves are growing out.

Orange blossoms are famous for evoking memories,[1] but the fragrance of plum blossoms above all makes us return to the past and remember nostalgically long-ago events. Nor can we overlook the clean loveliness of the *yamabuki*[2] or the uncertain beauty of wisteria, and so many other compelling sights.

Someone once remarked, "In summer,[3] when the Feast of Anointing the Buddha[4] and the Kamo Festival come around, and the young leaves on the treetops grow thick and cool, our sensitivity to the touching beauty of the world and our longing for absent friends grow stronger." Indeed, this is so. When, in the fifth month, the irises bloom and the rice seedlings are transplanted, can anyone remain untroubled by the drumming of the water rails? Then, in the sixth month, you can see the whiteness of moonflowers glowing over wretched hovels, and the smouldering of mosquito incense is affecting too. The purification rites of the sixth month[5] are also engrossing.

The celebration of *Tanabata* is charming.[6] Then, as the nights gradually become cold and the wild geese cry, the under leaves of the *hagi*[7] turn yellow, and men harvest and dry the first crop of rice. So many moving sights come together, in autumn especially. And how unforgettable is the morning after an equinoctal storm!—As I go on I realize that these sights have long since been enumerated in *The Tale of Genji* and *The Pillow Book,* but I make no pretense of trying to avoid saying the same things again. If I fail to say what lies on my mind it gives me a feeling of flatulence; I shall therefore give my brush free rein. Mine is a foolish diversion, but these pages are meant to be torn up, and no one is likely to see them.

To return to the subject. Winter decay is hardly less beautiful than autumn. Crimson leaves lie scattered on the grass beside the ponds, and how delightful it is on a morning when the frost is very white to see the vapor rise from a garden stream. At the end of the year it is indescribably moving to see everyone hurrying about on errands. There is something forlorn about the waning winter moon, shining cold and clear in the sky, unwatched because it is said to be depressing.[8] The Invocation of the Buddha Names and the departure of the messengers with the imperial offerings[9] are moving and inspiring. How impressive it is that so many palace ceremonials are performed besides all the preparations for the New Year! It is striking that the Worship of the Four Directions follows directly on the Expulsion of the Demons.[10]

On the last night of the year, when it is extremely dark, people light pine torches and go rushing about, pounding on the gates of strangers until well after midnight. I wonder what it signifies. After they have done with their exaggerated shouting and running so furiously that their feet hardly touch the ground, the noise at last fades away with the coming of the dawn, leaving a lonely feeling of regret over the departing old year. The custom of paying homage to the dead,[11] in the belief that they return that night, has lately disappeared from the capital, but I was deeply moved to discover that it was still performed in the East. As the day thus breaks on the New Year the sky seems no different from what it was the day before, but one feels somehow changed and renewed. The main thoroughfares, decorated their full length with pine boughs, seem cheerful and festive, and this too is profoundly affecting.

1. The scent of orange (*tachibana*) blossoms was believed to bring back old memories.
2. Sometimes translated as kerria roses, a yellow flower.
3. Kenkō's description shifts here from sights of spring to those of summer. I have inserted the word "summer" for clarity.
4. On the eighth day of the fourth month, the birthday of Shakyamuni, his statues were anointed with perfumed water. The Kamo Festival was held in the middle of the fourth month. Both were summer events because, in the lunar calendar, summer began with the fourth month.
5. On the last day of the sixth month, the last day of summer, palace officials sent little floats down the Kamo River, intended to symbolize sins accumulated during the year.
6. At this point the description shifts to autumn. *Tanabata,* a feast celebrated on the seventh night of the seventh month, commemorated the annual meeting of two stars.
7. The *lespedeza bicolor,* a lavender or white flower traditionally associated with the season of autumn rains. The turning of the colors of its under leaves is often mentioned in poetry as a sign of approaching winter.
8. Sei Shōnagon, in *The Pillow Book,* was one of many who found the late winter moon depressing.
9. For three days, beginning on the nineteenth of the twelfth month, rites were performed at the Seiryōden to purify the sins of the six senses. The names of the Buddhas of the Three Worlds were invoked.
   Messengers were sent from the provinces in the middle of the twelfth month with offerings of the harvest for the imperial tombs.
10. The Expulsion of the Demons (*tsuina*) took place on the last day of the year. The next morning, the emperor worshiped the Four Directions and the imperial tombs, and prayed for a safe and prosperous year.
11. The last night was one of six times during the year when the dead were believed to return. The Bon Festival preserves that belief today.

20

A certain hermit once said, "There is one thing that even I, who have no worldly entanglements, would be sorry to give up, the beauty of the sky." I can understand why he should have felt that way.

21

Looking at the moon is always diverting, no matter what the circumstances. A certain man once said, "Surely nothing is so delightful as the moon," but another man rejoined, "The dew moves me even more." How amusing that they should have argued the point! What could fail to be affecting in its proper season? This is obviously true of the moon and cherry blossoms. The wind seems to have a special power to move men's hearts.

Regardless of the season, however, a clear-flowing stream breaking against rocks makes a splendid sight. I remember how touched I was when I read the Chinese poem, "The Yüan and Hsiang[1] flow ever east, night and day alike; they never stop an instant to soothe the grieving man." Chi K'ang[2] also has the lines, "The heart rejoices to visit mountains and lakes and see the birds and fish." Nothing gives so much pleasure as to wander to some spot far from the world, where the water and vegetation are unsullied.

1. From a poem by Tai Shu-lun in the collection *San-t'i-shih* compiled by Chou Pi in 1250. This anthology of middle and late T'ang poetry was probably introduced to Japan before 1314. The poem cited describes the poet's emotions on visiting Hang-chou, far from the capital. Yüan and Hsiang are the names of rivers.
2. Hsi K'ang (223–62) was one of the Seven Sages of the Bamboo Grove. The poem paraphrased here is found in *Wen Hsüan*.

22

In all things I yearn for the past. Modern fashions seem to keep on growing more and more debased. I find that even among the splendid pieces of furniture built by our master cabinetmakers,[1] those in the old forms are the most pleasing. And as for writing letters, surviving scraps from the past reveal how superb the phrasing used to be. The ordinary spoken language has also steadily coarsened. People used to say "raise the carriage shafts" or "trim the lamp wick," but people today say "raise it" or "trim it." When they should say, "Let the men of the palace staff[2] stand forth!" they say, "Torches! Let's have some light!"[3] Instead of calling the place where the lectures on the Sutra of the Golden Light[4] are delivered before the emperor "the Hall of the Imperial Lecture," they shorten it to "the Lecture Hall," a deplorable corruption, an old gentleman complained.

1. This is apparently a reference to *Genji Monogatari*; it might therefore be better to translate *kano ki no michi no takumi* as "that [well-known] master cabinetmaker."
2. *Tonomoryō* is translated by R. K. Reischauer as "Bureau of Palace Equipment and Upkeep."
3. Kenkō contrasts the old, oblique command and the present, direct one.
4. The full title of the sutra in Japanese is *Konkōmyō Saishōō-kyō* (Sutra of the excellent golden light). It was the most influential Buddhist text in eighth-century Japan, and in Kenkō's day lectures on it were delivered at the palace in the fifth month every year.

23

They speak of the degenerate, final phase of the world, yet how splendid is the ancient atmosphere, uncontaminated by the world, that still prevails within the palace walls. The

Dew Terrace,[1] the Morning Collation, the This Hall, the That Gate—all have an impressive ring. Even objects that might equally well be found in some humble place, such as half-windows and blinds, a verandah of small boards, or a tall sliding door, sound quite splendid when the term is used of the palace.

It is particularly impressive when the cry goes up in the antechamber, "Prepare for night!"[2] It is pleasing too that they should call for the lanterns in His Majesty's bedchamber, "Light the lamps quickly!" The looks of smug competence on the faces of even minor officials of the palace staff, to say nothing of the great nobles performing official functions in council, are amusing. I was particularly entertained one extremely cold winter night to see these functionaries dozing through the ceremonies at their stations here and there in the hall. The Tokudaiji prime minister[3] once remarked that the dancers' bells in the Hall of the Sacred Mirror[4] had a lovely, noble sound.

1. This and the following are the names of a passageway and a room in the palace.
2. It is possible also to translate this as "Prepare the antechamber for night!" The antechamber (*jin*) was where nobles sat during a ceremony.
3. Fujiwara no Kintaka (1253–1305), who became prime minister in 1302.
4. *Naishidokoro,* where the Sacred Mirror, one of the three imperial regalia, was kept. Also called *Kashikodokoro.*

24

I believe that the most charming and touching sight is the Shrine in the Fields[1] when an imperial princess[2] is in residence. It is amusing how the people there avoid Buddhist words like "sutra" or "Buddha" and speak instead of "colored paper" or "the One inside." [3] Shinto shrines as a rule are too charming to pass without stopping. There is something peculiarly affecting about the atmosphere of their ancient groves, and how could the buildings, surrounded by a vermilion fence with sacred streamers tied to the *sakaki*[4] boughs, fail to impress? Especially splendid are Ise, Kamo, Kasuga, Hirano, Sumiyoshi, Miwa, Kibune, Yoshida, Ōharano, Matsunoo, and Umenomiya.

1. Nonomiya, a shrine in the Saga area, west of Kyoto. It is famous as the scene of the *Sakaki* chapter of *Genji Monogatari* and of the Nō play *Nonomiya*.

2. An imperial princess (*saiō* or *itsuki no miko*) was sent at the beginning of each reign, after the coronation of the new emperor, as a kind of vestal virgin to the shrine at Ise. She normally spent one year at the Shrine in the Fields before going on to Ise. Before leaving, she met the emperor at the imperial council hall (*Daigokuden*) and he passed a comb through her hair as a token of parting for life. As long as the emperor lived the princess could not marry or return to the capital. Kenkō probably refers here to the Princess Shōshi, the eldest daughter of the Emperor Go-Nijō, who went to the Shrine in the Fields in 1307.

3. *Nakago* (the One inside) may mean a Buddhist image inside its shrine, or else the middle image in a Buddhist trinity.

4. *Sakaki*, the *cleyera ochnacea*, is an evergreen of the camellia family. It is the sacred tree of Shinto and used in religious ceremonies.

25

The world is as unstable as the pools and shallows of Asuka River.[1] Times change and things disappear: joy and sorrow come and go;[2] a place that once thrived turns into an uninhabited moor; a house may remain unaltered, but its occupants will have changed. The peach and the damson trees in the garden say nothing[3]—with whom is one to reminisce about the past? I feel this sense of impermanence even more sharply when I see the remains of a house which long ago, before I knew it, must have been imposing.

Whenever I pass by the ruins of the Kyōgoku Palace,[4] the Hōjōji,[5] and similar buildings, it moves me to think that the aspiration of the builders still lingers on, though the edifices themselves have changed completely. When Fujiwara no Michinaga erected so magnificent a temple, bestowing many estates for its support, he supposed that his descendants would always assist the emperor and serve as pillars of the state; could he have imagined that the temple would fall into such ruin, no matter what times lay ahead? The Great Gate and the Golden Hall were still standing until recent years, but the Gate burned during the Shōwa era,[6] and the Golden Hall soon afterwards fell over. It still lies there, and no attempt has been made to restore it. Only the Muryōju Hall [7] remains as a memento of the temple's former glory. Nine images of Amida Buddha,[8] each sixteen feet tall,[9] stand in a row, most awesomely. It is extremely moving to see, still plainly visible, the plaque inscribed by the Major Counselor Kōzei[10] and the door inscription by Kaneyuki. I understand that the Hokke Hall [11] and perhaps other buildings are still standing. I wonder how much longer they too will last?

Some buildings that lack even such remains may survive merely as foundation stones, but no one knows for certain to what they once belonged. It is true in all things that it is a futile business attempting to plan for a future one will never know.

1. The Asuka River, a stream near Nara, figures prominently in Japanese poetry. Reference is made here to the anonymous poem in *Kokinshū*, "In this world what is constant? In the Asuka River yesterday's pools are today's shallows."
2. These phrases are borrowed from the Japanese preface to *Kokinshū*.

3. From a Chinese poem by Sugawara no Fumitoki (899–981) found in *Wakan Rōei Shū*.
4. The palace of the great statesman Fujiwara no Michinaga (966–1027).
5. Michinaga lived in this temple after retiring from public office in 1018.
6. The era lasted from 1312 to 1317. The date of the burning of the Gate is not known.
7. The formal name of the Amida Hall within the Hōjōji. It burnt in 1331, evidence that Kenkō wrote this section before then.
8. Each statue represented one level of Paradise.
9. Sixteen feet (*jōroku*) was the legendary height of the Buddha.
10. Fujiwara no Yukinari (972–1027), known by his artistic name of Kōzei, was a celebrated calligrapher.
11. A building used for contemplation on the Lotus Sutra by Tendai priests.

26

When I recall the months and years I spent as the intimate of someone whose affections have now faded like cherry blossoms scattering even before a wind blew, I still remember every word of hers that once so moved me; and when I realize that she, as happens in such cases, is steadily slipping away from my world, I feel a sadness greater even than that of separation from the dead. That is why, I am sure, a man once grieved that white thread should be dyed in different colors, and why another lamented that roads inevitably fork.[1] Among the hundred verses presented to the Retired Emperor Horikawa[2] one runs:

mukashi mishi	The fence round her house,
imo ga kakine wa	The woman I loved long ago,
arenikeri	Is ravaged and fallen;
tsubana majiri no	Only violets remain
sumire no mi shite	Mingled with the spring weeds.[3]

[27]

What a lonely picture—the poem must describe something that really occurred.[4]

1. The passage comes from the *Huai-nan Tzu*: "Yang-tzu saw a forked road and grieved that it would branch south and north. Mo-tzu saw raw silk and wept at the thought that some would be dyed yellow and some black. Kao Yu said, 'They were sad because what originally had been the same would now be different.' "
2. *Horikawa In Ontoki Hyakushu Waka* consists of poems by Fujiwara no Kinsada (1049–99) and others, a selection of the hundred best of 1,600 composed. It was compiled between 1099 and 1103.
3. The poem is by Fujiwara no Kinsada.
4. Modern scholarship indicates that Kinsada derived the poem from one by Ōtomo no Yakamochi, throwing doubt on the genuineness of his feelings.

27

The moment during the ceremony of abdication of the throne when the Sword, Jewels, and Mirror[1] are offered to the new emperor is heartbreaking in the extreme. When the newly retired emperor[2] abdicated in the spring [of 1318] he wrote this poem, I understand:

tonomori no	Even menials
tomo no miyakko	Of the palace staff treat me
yoso ni shite	As a stranger now;
harawanu niwa ni	In my unswept garden lie
hana zo chirishiku	The scattered cherry blossoms.[3]

What a lonely feeling the poem seems to convey—people are too distracted by all the festivities of the new reign for anyone to wait on the retired emperor. This is precisely the kind of occasion when a man's true feelings are apt to be revealed.

1. The three imperial regalia.
2. The Emperor Hanazono was known as the "newly retired emperor" (*shin-in*) from 1318 to 1333.
3. This poem, not preserved elsewhere, seems to derive from one by Minamoto no Kintada (889–948) in the anthology *Shūishū*: "Menials of the palace staff—if you are sensitive, forbear this spring alone from morning sweeping."

28

Nothing is more saddening than the year of imperial mourning. The very appearance of the temporary palace[1] is forbidding: the wooden floor built close to the ground, the crudely fashioned reed-blinds, the coarse, grey cloth hung above the blinds, the utensils of rough workmanship, and the attendants all wearing strangely drab costumes, sword scabbards, and sword knots.

1. The emperor moved to a temporary palace during the year of mourning for one of his parents.

29

When I sit down in quiet meditation, the one emotion hardest to fight against is a longing in all things for the past. After the others have gone to bed, I pass the time on a long autumn's night by putting in order whatever belongings are at hand. As I tear up scraps of old correspondence I should prefer not to leave behind, I sometimes find among them samples of the calligraphy of a friend who has died, or pictures he drew for his own amusement, and I feel exactly as I did at the time. Even with letters written by friends who are still alive I try, when it has been long since we met, to remember the circumstances, the year. What a moving experience that is! It is sad to think that a man's familiar possessions, indifferent to his death, should remain unaltered long after he is gone.

30

Nothing is sadder than the time after a death. During the forty-nine days of mourning[1] the family, having moved to a temple in the mountains or some such place, forgathers in large numbers in inconvenient, cramped quarters, and frantically occupies itself with the motions of mourning for the dead. The days pass unbelievably fast. On the final day, all civility gone, no one has a word for anybody else, and each man, with airs of knowing exactly what is to be done,[2] sets about packing his belongings; then all go their separate ways. Once they have returned home, many sad remembrances are sure to afflict them anew.

Sometimes I hear people say on such occasions, "It's bad luck to mention such and such a thing.[3] You should avoid it, for the family's sake." How can people worry about such things in the midst of so great a tragedy? The insensitivity of people still appalls me.

We do not by any means forget the dead, even after months and years have gone by, but, as they say, "the departed one grows more distant each day." We may deny it, but—no doubt because our sorrow is not as sharp as at the time—we talk about foolish things, we smile.

The body is interred in some lonely mountain and visited only at the required times. Before long, the grave marker is covered with moss and buried in fallen leaves. The evening storms and the night moon become the only regular mourners.

As long as people remember the deceased person and miss him, all is still well, but before long those people too disappear, and the descendants, who know the man only from reports, are hardly likely to feel deep emotion. Once the services honoring the dead man cease, nobody knows who he was or even his name. Only the sight of the spring weeds sprouting each year by his grave will stir the emotions of sensitive people; but in the end, even the pine tree that groaned in the storm winds is broken into firewood before it reaches its allotted thousand years, and the old grave is plowed up and turned into rice land. How sad it is that even this last memento of the dead should vanish.

1. The *chūin* period when the soul of a deceased person waits for the form it will assume in the next life. The family prays that he will be reborn in desirable circumstances.
2. *Ware kashikoge ni* is ambiguous. Other interpretations include: "each, thinking of his own convenience"; "each with an air of showing the others he can cope efficiently"; "in a most businesslike manner," etc.
3. This refers to various superstitions, such as the belief that if a funeral takes place on a *tomobiki* day some other member of the family will also die.

3 1

One morning after a pleasant fall of snow I sent a letter to someone with whom I had business, but failed to mention the snow. The reply was amusing: "Do you suppose that I shall take any notice of what someone says who is so perverse that he writes a letter without a word of inquiry about how I am enjoying the snow? I am most disappointed in you." Now that the author of that letter is dead, even so trivial an incident sticks in my mind.

32

About the twentieth of the ninth month, at the invitation of a certain gentleman, I spent the night wandering with him viewing the moon. He happened to remember a house we passed on the way, and, having himself announced, went inside. In a corner of the overgrown garden heavy with dew, I caught the faint scent of some perfume which seemed quite accidental. This suggestion of someone living in retirement from the world moved me deeply.

In due time, the gentleman emerged, but I was still under the spell of the place. As I gazed for a while at the scene from the shadows, someone pushed the double doors open a crack wider, evidently to look at the moon. It would have been most disappointing if she had bolted the doors as soon as he had gone! How was she to know that someone lingering behind would see her? Such a gesture could only have been the product of inborn sensitivity.

I heard that she died not long afterwards.

33

When construction of the present palace[1] had been completed, the buildings were inspected by experts on court usage, who pronounced them free of faults anywhere. The day for the emperor to move to the new palace was already near when the Abbess Genki[2] examined it and declared, "The bell-shaped windows in the Kan'in palace[3] were rounder and without frames." This was an impressive feat of memory. The windows in the new palace, peaked at the top, had wooden borders. This mistake was later corrected.

1. Completed in 1317, during the reign of the Emperor Hanazono. It burnt in 1336.
2. Fujiwara no Inshi (1246–1317), the consort of the Emperor Go-Fukakusa and mother of the Emperor Fushimi.
3. The palace used by ten sovereigns from Takakura to Go-Fukakusa. It burnt in 1259, when the Abbess Genki was only thirteen.

34

The *kaikō* is the lid of a shell resembling the conch, but smaller and with a long, narrow projection at the mouth. I found some at the Bay of Kanesawa in Musashi Province.[1] The people of the place call it *henatari*.

1. The area today is inside the city of Yokohama.

35

A person with a bad handwriting should not be embarrassed to write his own letters. There is something irritating about people who, pleading their writing is ugly, ask others to write for them.

36

Someone once told me this story. "I had failed to visit a certain lady for a long time, and, being aware of my negligence, I could imagine how annoyed she must be with me. I felt there was nothing I could say by way of apology. Just at this time a most unexpected and welcome message came from the lady asking, 'Have you a workman you can spare?' That is the kind of disposition I admire in a woman." I was struck by the aptness of his remark.

37

When a person who has always been extremely close appears on a particular occasion reserved and formal towards you, some people undoubtedly will say, "Why act that way now, after all these years?" But I feel that such behavior shows sincerity and breeding.

On the other hand, I am sure I should feel equally attracted if someone with whom I am on distant terms should choose on some occasion to speak to me with utter frankness.

38

What a foolish thing it is to be governed by a desire for fame and profit and to fret away one's whole life without a moment of peace. Great wealth is no guarantee of security. Wealth, in fact, tends to attract calamities and disaster. Even if, after you die, you leave enough gold to prop up the North Star,[1] it will only prove a nuisance to your heirs. The pleasures that delight the foolish man are likewise meaningless to the man of discrimination who considers a big carriage, sleek horses, gold, and jeweled ornaments all equally undesirable and senseless. You had best throw away your gold in the mountains and drop your jewels into a ravine. It is an exceedingly stupid man who will torment himself for the sake of worldly gain.

To leave behind a reputation that will not perish through long ages to come is certainly to be desired, but can one say that men of high rank and position are necessarily superior? There are foolish and incompetent men who, having been born into an illustrious family and, being favored by the times, rise to exalted position and indulge themselves in the extremes of luxury. There are also many learned and good men who by their own choice remain in humble positions and end their days without ever having encountered good fortune. A feverish craving for high rank and position is second in foolishness only to seeking wealth.

One would like to leave behind a glorious reputation for surpassing wisdom and character, but careful reflection will show that what we mean by love of a glorious reputation is delight in the approbation of others. Neither those who praise nor those who abuse last for long, and the people who have heard their reports are likely to depart the world as quickly. Before whom then should we feel ashamed? By whom should we wish to be appreciated? Fame, moreover, inspires backbiting. It does no good whatsoever to have one's name survive. A craving after fame is next most foolish.

If I were to address myself to those who nevertheless seek desperately to attain knowledge and wisdom, I would say that knowledge leads to deceit, and artistic talent is the product of much suffering. True knowledge is not what one hears from others or acquires through study. What, then, are we to call knowledge? Proper and improper come to one and the same thing—can we call anything "good"? [2] The truly enlightened man has no learning, no virtue, no accomplishments, no fame. [3] Who knows of him, who will report his glory? It is not that he conceals his virtue or pretends to be stupid; it is because from the outset he is above distinctions between wise and foolish, between profit and loss.

If, in your delusion, you seek fame and profit, the results will be as I have described. All is unreality. Nothing is worth discussing, worth desiring.

1. The phrase is borrowed from a poem by Po Chü-i containing the lines, "Even if, by the time you die, you have amassed gold enough to support the North Star, it is not as good as having a cask of wine while you are alive."
2. The expression is from Chuang Tzu, the Taoist philosopher, whose works were widely read by Zen monks of Kenkō's time.
3. This sentence too is from Chuang Tzu.

39

A certain man once asked the High Priest Hōnen,[1] "Sometimes as I am saying the *nembutsu*[2] I am seized by drowsiness and I neglect my devotions. How can I overcome this obstacle?" Hōnen replied, "Say the *nembutsu* as long as you are awake." This was a most inspiring answer. Again, he said, "If you are certain you will go to heaven, you certainly will; if you are uncertain, it is uncertain." This too was a sage remark. Again, he said, "Even if you have doubts, you will go to heaven provided you say the *nembutsu*." This too was a holy utterance.

1. Hōnen Shōnin (1133–1212) was the Japanese founder of the Jōdo (Pure Land) sect of Buddhism.
2. Jōdo Buddhists believe that salvation may be obtained by calling on Amida Buddha. This is known as *nembutsu*.

40

The daughter of a certain lay priest in the province of Inaba was reputed to be very beautiful, and many suitors asked for her hand, but this girl ate nothing but chestnuts, and refused to touch rice or other grains. Her father therefore declined the men's proposals, saying, "Such a peculiar person is not fit to be married."

41

On the fifth day of the fifth month I went to see the horse race at the Kamo Shrine.[1] There was such a mob before our carriage, between us and the view, that we could see nothing. We all got out of the carriage and pushed towards the railing, but the crowd was particularly dense in that area, and there seemed no chance of making our way to the fore. Just then we noticed a priest perched in the crotch of an *ōchi*[2] tree across the way, watching the race. Even as he clung to the tree he was nodding drowsily, again and again waking himself just as he seemed about to fall.

People, observing the priest, laughed at his folly. "What an idiot! Imagine anyone being able to sleep so peacefully when he's sitting on such a dangerous branch!" It suddenly occurred to me, however, "The hour of death may be upon us at any moment. To spend our days in pleasure-seeking, forgetful of this truth, is even more foolish." I blurted out the words, and some people standing before me said, "That's certainly true. It is a most stupid way to behave." Turning round towards us, they said, "Please come through here," and made room, urging us to take their places.

Anybody at all might have made the same observation, but probably it came as a surprise at that particular moment and struck home. Man, not being made of wood or stone, is at times not without emotional reactions.

1. A feature of the Kamo Festival is the horse race from the first to the second *torii* of the Upper Kamo Shrine.
2. The azedarach, also called bead tree, etc.

42

The monk called the Abbot Gyōga,[1] the son of the Karahashi middle commander,[2] was a teacher of religious doctrine. He suffered from dizzy spells and gradually, as he advanced in years, his nose stopped up, and he had difficulty in breathing. He underwent all kinds of treatment, but his ailment grew only the worse. His eyes, brows, and forehead swelled horribly and bulged out so much he could not even see. At first his face looked rather like a *ninomai*[3] mask, but eventually it became quite terrifying, like a devil's face. His eyes were stuck to the top of his head, what had been his forehead became his nose, and so on. After this, he no longer showed himself even before the other priests of the temple, but remained in complete seclusion. Many years went by in this fashion, but finally his condition grew even worse and he died. Such sicknesses actually exist.

1. Gyōga Sōzu. Nothing is known about him. The rank *sōzu* was fourth highest in the hierarchy of Buddhist priests.
2. Minamoto no Masakiyo (1182–1230).
3. *Ninomai* is a variety of *bugaku* dance. One of the masks used in the dance has grotesquely swollen brows that puff out over the eyes.

43

Towards the end of spring, on a lovely, mild day, I strolled by a stately-looking mansion set on a large property with ancient trees. A cherry tree was shedding blossoms in the garden. It was impossible to pass without stopping, and I went in. The shutters on the south side were all lowered and the place looked deserted, but I could see then, through an opening in the bamboo blinds over double doors that faced east and had been left attractively ajar, a handsome young man of about twenty, at his ease but maintaining an elegant composure. He was reading a book he held open before him on a desk. I wonder who he was. I should like to visit him and ask.

44

A very young man, attired with great distinction in a glittering tunic—I could not make out the coloring in the moonlight—and trousers of a dark purple, stepped from the roughly made door of woven bamboo and, accompanied by a small boy, made his way along a path through ricefields that stretched into the distance. Drenched though he was by dew from the leaves of rice plants, he amused himself as he went along by playing a flute with consummate skill. I was curious to know where he might be headed, thinking it unlikely anyone here could appreciate such playing, and followed him. Presently, the man stopped playing his flute and, as he reached the foot of the hill, entered a mansion with an imposing gate. I could see a carriage with its shafts resting on a stand in the courtyard, looking far more conspicuous than it would have in the capital. I asked a servant why it was there and he replied, "A certain prince is residing here now. I imagine there is to be a Buddhist service."

Priests had assembled at the family chapel. A penetrating fragrance of incense wafted towards me in the cold night air. Ladies in waiting traversed the corridor leading from the residence to the chapel, leaving in their wake a fragrance of perfumed robes. Such attention to elegance of person was surprising in a mountain village, where none would see them.

The garden, like an autumn field left to grow wild, was buried in dew so heavy it spilled from the plants. The cries of the insects had a plaintive note; a garden stream murmured gently.

The clouds passing to and fro seemed to move more quickly than in the capital, and the moon, never long the same, was clear and clouded by turns.

45

Kin'yo,[1] an officer of the second rank, had a brother called the High Priest Ryōgaku,[2] an extremely bad-tempered man. Next to his monastery grew a large nettle-tree which occasioned the nickname people gave him, the Nettle-tree High Priest. "That name is outrageous," said the high priest, and cut down the tree. The stump still being left, people referred to him now as the Stump High Priest. More furious than ever, Ryōgaku had the stump dug up and thrown away, but this left a big ditch. People now called him the Ditch High Priest.

1. Fujiwara no Kin'yo (died 1301) was a poet.
2. Ryōgaku Sōjō (died about 1305) was a distinguished poet. He is here called *sōjō*, but elsewhere is referred to as *daisōjō*, a position at the top of the Buddhist hierarchy.

46

The priest known as the Burglar Bishop[1] lived near Yanagihara. His frequent encounters with burglars gave him the name, I understand.

1. *Hōin* was the highest rank of Buddhist priest, bestowed by the court.

47

A certain man on his way to Kiyomizu was joined on the road by an aged nun. As they trudged along, she kept murmuring, *"Kusame, kusame,"*[1] until finally he asked her, "Sister, why do you say that?" Without even deigning to answer, she kept up an unbroken stream of repetitions of the word. He persisted, and when she had been asked several times she at last became angry and said, "What a nuisance of a man! Don't you know that unless you say the magic word when somebody sneezes, he'll die? The young master I've brought up is an acolyte now on Mount Hiei. He may be sneezing at this very minute, for all I know. That's why I said *kusame*." This was certainly a case of unusual devotion.

1. The word *kusame* (*kushami* in modern Japanese) means a sneeze, but is here used to ward off the dangers of a sneeze, much in the manner of "God bless you!"

48

When Lord Mitsuchika[1] was serving as supervisor of the
lectures on the Sutra of the Golden Light in the palace of the
cloistered emperor,[2] he was summoned before His Majesty,
who offered food from his own tray and invited Mitsuchika
to eat. When Mitsuchika had hastily finished the meal, he
pushed the stand behind the imperial screen of state, and
took his leave. The ladies in waiting cried out to each other,
"Ugh! How dirty! Does he expect us to clean up his mess?"[3]
But the cloistered emperor exclaimed in great admiration,
"That is how a man familiar with precedent behaves! I am
most impressed."

1. Fujiwara no Mitsuchika (1176–1221), a model statesman, who unsuccessfully attempted to dissuade the Emperor Go-Toba from plotting
   against the Hōjō regents, was executed during the war.
2. The Cloistered Emperor Go-Toba. For the sutra, see above sec. 22, n. 4.
3. The word *tore* is here interpreted as meaning "clean up," but some
   scholars take it to mean "eat"—that is, "Does he expect us to eat his
   left-overs?"

49

You must not wait until you are old before you begin practicing the Way. Most of the gravestones from the past belong
to men who died young.

A man sometimes learns for the first time how mistaken his
way of life has been only when he unexpectedly falls ill and
is about to depart this world. His mistake lay in doing
slowly what should have been done quickly, and in hasten-
ing to do what might best have been delayed.[1] He regrets
these actions committed in the past, but what good can it do,
even if he feels regret, at that stage?

A man should bear firmly in mind that death is always threatening, and never for an instant forget it. If he does this, why should the impurities bred in him by this world not grow lighter, and his heart not develop an earnest resolve to cultivate the Way of the Buddha? The story is told in Zenrin's *Ten Courses of Salvation*[2] of a holy man of long ago who, when someone came to discuss important business concerning them both, answered, "An extremely urgent matter has come up, and it must be settled by morning, if not tonight." So saying, he covered his ears, recited the *nembutsu,* and presently achieved Buddhahood.

A holy man named Shinkai[3] was so aware of the impermanence of the world that he never even sat down and relaxed, but always remained crouching.

1. This means he was slow to perform Buddhist duties but quick to indulge in worldly activities.
2. Zenrin is short for Zenrinji, a Jōdo temple in Kyoto north of Nanzenji. It refers here to a monk of that temple named Yōgan (1032–1111), known familiarly as Zenrin Yōgan. His work *Ōjō Jūin,* mentioned here, was widely read.
3. An adopted son of Taira no Munemori who, after the defeat of his clan, took refuge on Mount Kōya, the center of Shingon Buddhism.

50

Along about the Ōchō era[1] there was a rumor that a man from Ise had brought to the capital a woman who had become a demon, and for twenty days or more people of the downtown and Shirakawa areas wandered here and there day after day, hoping for a look at the demon. They passed the word to one another: "Yesterday she visited the Saionji.[2] Today she's sure to go to the cloistered emperor's palace. At the moment she's at such and such a place." Nobody actually claimed to have seen the demon, but no one, for that matter, said the report was untrue. People of all classes gossiped continuously about one subject, the demon—that, and nothing else.

One day, as I was on my way from Higashiyama to the area around Agui, I saw a crowd of people running from Shijō and above, all headed north. They were shouting that the demon had been seen at the corner of Ichijō and Muromachi. I looked off in that direction from where I was, near Imadegawa. There was such a crowd packed around the cloistered emperor's reviewing stand[3] that it seemed quite impossible to get through. I thought it unlikely the rumor could be completely groundless, and sent a man to investigate, but he could find nobody who had actually met the demon. The crowd continued to clamor in this manner until it grew dark. Finally, quarrels broke out and a number of unpleasant incidents occurred. For some time afterward, whenever anyone took sick for a few days, people tended to say that the false rumors about the demon had been a portent of the illness.

1. The era lasted from 1311 to 1312. The event probably occurred when Kenkō was twenty-eight, in 1311.
2. A temple northwest of Kyoto, near the Kinkakuji. The branch of the Fujiwara family residing there became known as Saionji.
3. A stand used by the cloistered emperor when watching the Kamo Festival.

5 1

The cloistered emperor, having decided to introduce water from the Ōi River into the pond of his Kameyama palace,[1] commanded the inhabitants of Ōi to build a waterwheel. He paid them generously, and the men worked hard for several days to construct it. But when the wheel was put in place it failed to turn at all. The men tried in various ways to repair it, but it stood there useless, stubbornly refusing to turn. The emperor thereupon summoned some villagers from Uji and ordered them to build a waterwheel. They put one together without difficulty and presented it. The wheel turned perfectly and was splendidly efficient at drawing up water.

Expert knowledge in any art is a noble thing.

1. This detached palace, used by the Cloistered Emperors Go-Saga (1220–72) and Kameyama (1249–1305), stood near the present Tenryūji, west of Kyoto. The Ōi River flows nearby at Arashiyama. The cloistered emperor of this episode could be either Go-Saga or Kameyama.

52

A certain priest in the Ninnaji,[1] regretting that he had never worshiped at Iwashimizu,[2] though now advanced in years, made up his mind one day and set off alone on foot on his pilgrimage. He worshiped at the Gokuraku temple and the Kōra shrine and, supposing that was all there was to Iwashimizu,[3] returned to the Ninnaji. Back in his temple, he told his fellow priests, "I've succeeded in realizing my dreams of many years. The shrine was even more impressive than I had been led to believe. But I wonder why the other pilgrims all climbed the mountain. Is there something there? I wanted to have a look for myself, but my main object, after all, was to worship the god, so I decided not to explore the mountain." Even in trivial matters a guide is desirable.

1. An important monastery of Shingon Buddhism situated northwest of Kyoto.
2. A Shinto shrine dedicated to Hachiman, situated between Kyoto and Osaka.
3. The priest visited two minor buildings, but did not realize that the main part of the shrine was on the mountain.

53

This story too is about a priest at the Ninnaji. A farewell party was being offered for an acolyte about to become a priest, and the guests were all making merry when one of the priests, drunk and carried away by high spirits, picked up a three-legged cauldron nearby, and clamped it over his head. It caught on his nose, but he flattened it down, pulled the pot over his face, and danced out among the others, to the great amusement of everyone.

After the priest had been dancing for a while he tried to pull the pot off, but it refused to be budged. A pall fell over the gathering, and people wondered blankly what to do. They tried one thing and another, only succeeding in bruising the skin around his neck. The blood streamed down, and the priest's neck became so swollen that he had trouble breathing. The others tried to split the pot, but it was not easily broken and the reverberations inside were unbearable. Finally, when all else had failed, they threw a thin garment over the legs of the pot, which stuck up like horns, and, giving the priest a stick to lean on, led him off by the hand to a doctor in Kyoto. People they met on the way stared at this apparition with unconstrained astonishment.

The priest presented a most extraordinary sight as he sat inside the doctor's office facing him. Whatever he said came out as an unintelligible, muffled roar. "I can't find any similar case in my medical books," said the doctor, "and there aren't any oral traditions either." The priest had no choice but to return to the Ninnaji, where his close friends and his aged mother gathered at his bedside, weeping with grief, though the priest himself probably could not hear them.

At this point somebody suggested, "Wouldn't it be better at least to save his life, even if he loses his nose and ears? Let's try pulling the pot off with all our strength." They stuffed straw around the priest's neck to protect it from the metal, then pulled hard enough to tear off his head. Only holes were left to show where his ears and nose had been, but the pot was removed. They barely managed to save the priest's life, and for a long time afterwards he was gravely ill.

54

There was a ravishing acolyte at Omuro,[1] and various priests were scheming how they might inveigle him into going out with them. They enlisted the help of some talented entertainers[2] who carefully prepared an elegant hamper and fitted it into a kind of box which they buried in the ground at a pleasant spot not far from Narabigaoka.[3] The priests, after scattering autumn leaves over the place so that no one would guess anything lay buried there, returned to Omuro and induced the boy to accompany them on the picnic. The priests, delighted with their success, tramped around the neighborhood with the boy until they came near the mossy spot where the box was buried. There they sat themselves in a row. "I'm absolutely exhausted," said one priest. "I wish

"This story too is about a priest at the Ninnaji. . . .
[He] picked up a three-legged cauldron . . ."

仁和寺の童は師よりんとする
名おくて各あそぶり者けふ
酔く酔て入すぐ久を飯く
りらにろざにはるゆり
との紙鼻をとり
さくかふを
床あるふまんぞ
む入へくきしいを
しる

there were somebody to burn autumn leaves!"[4] said another. "Why don't you miracle-working priests try praying?" asked a third. The priests, rubbing their rosaries and elaborately describing magic gestures with their fingers, started to walk towards the tree beneath which the treasure lay buried. After this extraordinary performance they scraped away the leaves, to find nothing. Thinking they might have mistaken the place, they roamed over the whole mountain leaving nowhere undug, but still there was nothing. Someone had observed them burying the hamper and stolen it while they were off in Omuro. The priests, for a time at a loss for words, presently fell to quarreling most unpleasantly, and returned in a rage to the temple. Any excessively ingenious scheme is sure to end in a fiasco.

1. Omuro was another name for the Ninnaji.
2. *Asobi-hōshi* may originally have been priests who specialized in dancing and singing, but by this time *hōshi* included entertainers who dressed as priests without taking orders.
3. Narabigaoka is the name of three hills of similar shape in the west of Kyoto. Tradition has it that Kenkō lived here and that a tombstone at the foot of one hill marks his grave.
4. An allusion to lines in a poem by Po Chü-i quoted in *Wakan Rōei Shū*: "In the forest we warm our wine by burning crimson leaves; on the rock we write verses and brush away green moss." The lines were often alluded to in Japanese writings. The meaning here is, "I wish someone would warm saké for us!"

55

A house should be built with the summer in mind. In winter it is possible to live anywhere, but a badly made house is unbearable when it gets hot.

There is nothing cool-looking about deep water; a shallow, flowing stream is far cooler. When you are reading fine print you will find that a room with sliding doors is lighter than one with hinged shutters. A room with a high ceiling is cold in winter and dark by lamplight. People agree that a house which has plenty of spare room is attractive to look at and may be put to many different uses.

56

How boring it is when you meet a man after a long separation and he insists on relating at interminable length everything that has happened to him in the meantime. Even if the man is an intimate, somebody you know extremely well, how can you but feel a certain reserve on meeting him again after a time? The vulgar sort of person, even if he goes on a brief excursion somewhere, is breathless with excitement as he relates as matters of great interest everything that has happened to him. When the well-bred man tells a story he addresses himself to one person, even if many people are present, though the others too listen, naturally. But the ill-bred man flings out his words into the crowd, addressing himself to no one in particular, and describes what happened so graphically that everyone bursts into boisterous laughter. You can judge a person's breeding by whether he is quite impassive even when he tells an amusing story, or laughs a great deal even when relating a matter of no interest.

It is most distressing, when the good and bad of somebody's appearance or the quality of a certain person's scholarship is being evaluated, for the speaker to refer to himself by way of comparison.

57

It is exasperating when discussions of poetry are devoted to bad poems. How, one wonders, could anyone with the smallest knowledge of the art have supposed such verses were worthy of discussion?

Even to an outsider, it is both embarrassing and painful to listen to someone discuss a subject—whatever it may be —that he doesn't really know.

58

Some say, "As long as your mind is set on enlightenment, it does not make much difference where you live. Even if you live with your family and mingle in society, why should that interfere with your prayers for happiness in the future life?" Men who speak in such terms know nothing whatsoever about the meaning of prayers for the future life. Indeed, once a man realizes how fleeting this life is and resolves to escape at all costs from the cycle of birth and death, what pleasure can he take in daily attendance on some lord or in schemes to benefit his family? A man's mind is influenced by his environment, and unless he has peaceful surroundings he will have difficulty in carrying out his religious duties.

People today cannot compare in resourcefulness with men of the past. They go into the mountain forests to live as hermits, only to find the life unendurable without some means of allaying their hunger and shielding themselves from the storms. As a result, how can they help but display at times something akin to a craving for worldly goods?

But it would be absurd to conclude therefore: "There is no point in becoming a priest. If that is the best a man can do, why should he abandon the world?" Despite everything, once a man has entered the Way of the Buddha and turned his back on the world, even supposing he has desires, they cannot possibly resemble the deep-seated cravings of men in power. How much expense to society are his paper bedclothes, his hempen robe, a bowl of food, and some millet broth? His wants are easily met, his heart quickly satisfied. Since, moreover, he is in some sense ashamed of his appearance,[1] he obviously will most often stay away from evil and keep close to good. It is desirable somehow to make a break from this world so that one may benefit from having been born a man.[2] The man who surrenders himself to his desires and neglects the path of enlightenment is hardly any different from the brute beasts.

1. That is, being ashamed of his shaven head and black robes, he will avoid frivolous company.
2. One should take advantage of having been reborn as a man in this life to become a priest and thereby escape the cycle of rebirth.

59

A man who has determined to take the Great Step should leave unresolved all plans for disposing of urgent or worrisome business.

Some men think, "I'll wait a bit longer, until I take care of this matter," or "I might as well dispose of that business first," or "People will surely laugh at me if I leave such and such as it stands. I'll arrange things now so that there won't be any future criticism," or "I've managed to survive all these years. I'll wait till that matter is cleared up. It won't take long. I mustn't be hasty." But if you think in such terms the day for taking the Great Step will never come, for you will keep discovering more and more unavoidable problems, and there will never be a time when you run out of unfinished business.

My observation of people leads me to conclude, generally speaking, that even people with some degree of intelligence are likely to go through life supposing they have ample time before them. But would a man fleeing because a fire has broken out in his neighborhood say to the fire, "Wait a moment, please!"? To save his life, a man will run away, indifferent to shame, abandoning his possessions. Is a man's life any more likely to wait for him? Death attacks faster than fire or water, and is harder to escape. When its hour comes, can you refuse to give up your aged parents, your little children, your duty to your master, your affections for others, because they are hard to abandon?

60

Jōshin, an abbot of the Shinjō-in,[1] was a high-ranking priest of great holiness. He was extremely fond of what are known as "potato heads,"[2] and devoured prodigious quantities of them. He kept a large bowl heaped with these potatoes by his knee in his scripture class, and would go on eating as he lectured on the sacred books. If ever he fell ill he would shut himself up in his room for a week or a fortnight, announcing that he was taking a cure, and indulge himself with especially good potatoes, eating more than ever. This was how he cured any and all ailments. He never gave his potatoes to anyone else, but ate them all himself.

Jōshin had always been extremely poor, but his teacher on his deathbed left Jōshin 200 *kan*[3] of copper coins and a monks' residence hall. Jōshin sold the building for 100 *kan,* making a total of 30,000 *hiki,* all of which he decided to use for buying potatoes. He deposited the money with a man in the capital and had potatoes delivered to him in lots of 10 *kan* worth each. In this way he was able to eat all the potatoes he could desire, so many indeed that although he made no other use of the money, it soon disappeared. People said, "A poor man who falls heir to 300 *kan* and then spends it in that way must be pious indeed."

Once, when this abbot saw a certain priest, he dubbed him the *Shiroururi.*[4] Someone asked what a *shiroururi* was. He replied, "I have no idea, but if such a thing existed, I am sure it would look like that priest's face."

This abbot was handsome, robustly built, a great eater, and better than anyone at calligraphy, Buddhist scholarship, and rhetoric. He was highly regarded within his temple as a beacon of the sect, but, being an eccentric who cared nothing for society and acted exactly as he pleased in everything, he refused ever to conform to the others. Even when he sat down to a collation after performing a service, he would never wait until the others were served, but began eating by himself as soon as the food was put before him. Then, the moment he felt like leaving he would stand up from the table and go off by himself. He did not eat even collations in his temple at the regular times with the others, but whenever he felt like eating, whether in the middle of the night or at the break of day. When he felt like sleeping, he shut himself in his room, even in broad daylight, and refused to listen when

[55]

people addressed him, no matter how urgent their business might be. Once he awakened, he might then spend several nights without sleeping, going about serenely, whistling as he went. His behavior was unconventional, but people, far from disliking him, allowed him everything. Might it have been because his virtue had attained the highest degree?

1. A temple, part of the Ninnaji, where nobles who had become priests resided. Nothing is known about Jōshin.
2. *Imogashira,* apparently a kind of taro.
3. One *kan* of *zeni* (copper coins) equaled 100 *hiki* or 1,000 *mon. Zeni,* coins with square holes, were kept on strings of 100 or 1,000 coins.
4. The meaning of *shirouri* is not known. It has been suggested that it has no meaning though the sounds suggest something whitish (*shiro*) and glossy like lapis (*ruri*). The word also resembles *shirouri* (a white melon).

61

The custom of dropping a rice steamer[1] from the palace roof on the occasion of an imperial birth is not a regular practice. It is a kind of magic, resorted to when the afterbirth has been slow. Unless this occurs, the ceremony is not performed. The custom originated with the lower classes and has no real historical justification. The rice steamers are ordered from the village of Ōhara.[2] A painting, preserved in an old treasury, depicts a member of the lower classes dropping a rice steamer from the roof of a house where a child is being born.

1. The word *koshiki* (rice steamer) contains the word *koshi* (hips). It has been argued therefore that verbal magic was involved.
2. The name may be a pun on *ōhara* (big belly).

62

When the Princess Ensei[1] was a small child she asked some-one going to the cloistered emperor's palace to relay the fol-lowing poem as a message from her:

futatsu moji	The letter in two strokes,
ushi no tsuno moji	The letter like an ox's horns,
sugu no moji	The straight letter,
yugamu moji to zo	And the crooked letter too
kimi wa oboyuru	All spell my love for you.[2]

The poem means that she missed her father, the cloistered emperor.

1. Princess Esshi (1229–1332), the second daughter of the Emperor Go-Saga. Ensei was her Buddhist name.
2. These descriptions of the shapes of letters of the *hiragana* syllabary spell out the word *ko-i-shi-ku,* meaning "lovingly" or "longingly."

63

The use of soldiers to protect the Leader during the Second Week ceremonies[1] goes back to some time in the past when robbers interrupted the rites. The soldiers were known as "officers on watch" and their functions gradually developed into the present ritual. The auguries for the entire year are revealed by the conduct of these ceremonies, and the use of soldiers is therefore disturbing.

1. Ceremonies performed for seven days, beginning on the eighth day of the first month, at the Shingon-in, a temple within the palace. Prayers were offered by the Leader (*azari*), the senior priest of the Tōji, an-other Shingon temple.

64

A certain gentleman expressed the opinion that the use of five hanging straps on the blinds of a carriage is not necessarily the privilege of a particular class of person. Any man who has reached the highest rank to which his birth entitles him may ride in such a carriage.

65

Court caps in recent years have become much taller than formerly. People who own the old-fashioned boxes must add an extra lid to accommodate the new caps.

66

The chancellor from Okamoto[1] once gave Shimotsuke no Takekatsu, the master of falconry, a brace of pheasants and a branch of fully opened red plum blossoms with the command that he attach the birds to the branch. Takekatsu replied, "I do not know how to attach birds to a branch in blossom, nor do I know how to attach a pair to a single branch." The chancellor asked the palace chef and various other people if they knew the art, but finally he summoned Takekatsu again and said, "It looks as if no one else knows either. Attach the birds in whatever way you think best." Takekatsu attached one pheasant to a bare plum branch and offered this to the chancellor.

Takekatsu explained, "A pheasant may be attached to a

branch of brushwood or else to a plum branch, but if it is to a plum branch, only to one which is in bud or has lost its blossoms. It may also be attached to a five-needled pine. The branch should be seven or else six feet long. It is pointed by slashing downwards diagonally, then cutting upwards from the opposite side to a depth of half an inch. The pheasant is attached halfway along the branch. Sometimes the pheasant is attached by the head, sometimes by the feet. The bird should be fastened at two places with arrowroot vine that has not been split. The ends of the vine should be cut to the same length as the false wing[2] of the bird and twisted into the shape of an ox's horns. The branch, customarily presented on the morning of the first snow, is carried over the shoulder, and brought in through the central gate with appropriate ceremony. The messenger follows the stone pavement under the eaves, taking care not to leave footprints in the snow. He plucks a few of the downy rump feathers and scatters them, then leans the branch against the porch railing of the palace building. If a gift is bestowed,[3] he throws it over his shoulder, bows in gratitude and withdraws.

"Even if a snowfall is the first of the year, a pheasant should not be offered if the snow is too scant to cover the toes of the shoes. The rump feathers are scattered to suggest that the pheasant has been captured by an imperial falcon, since the falcon normally seizes its prey by the small of the back."

I wonder why a pheasant is not attached to a branch in flower. A passage in *Ise Monogatari*[4] tells how someone in early autumn once tied a pheasant to an artificial branch of plum and sent it with the poem, "These blossoms, that now I pluck for you, my lord, distinguish not the season."[5] I wonder if artificial flowers were not inappropriate.

1. Fujiwara no Iehira (1282–1324) served as chancellor (*kampaku*) from 1313 to 1315. Okamoto was northeast of Kyoto.
2. *Hiuchiba*, translated as "false wing," is conjectural. Some commentators say it is a small wing at the base of the "real wing."
3. The gift was presumably a garment.
4. A collection of stories about the celebrated poet and lover Ariwara no Narihira (825–80), written in the ninth century.
5. The poem is given somewhat differently in *Ise Monogatari* and *Kokin-shū*.

67

The Iwamoto and Hashimoto sanctuaries within the Kamo shrine are dedicated respectively to Narihira[1] and Sanekata.[2] People are constantly confusing the two. One year I visited the shrine and stopped an aged priest who was passing by to inquire about them. He answered, "They say that Sanekata's is at the place where he left his reflection in the sacred stream. Hashimoto is the closer of the two sanctuaries to the water, so I imagine that one is his. I have heard that the lines by the abbot from Yoshimizu,[3]

tsuki wo mede	That charming gentleman
hana wo nagameshi	Of ancient times who loved
inishie no	The moon and brooded
yasashiki hito wa	Over the cherry blossoms
koko ni ariwara	Lies here—Ariwara,[4]

refer to the Iwamoto shrine, but I am sure you are much better informed than we are."

I was impressed by his extremely deferential way of speaking.

The Lady Konoe,[5] who was in the service of the cloistered princess of Imadegawa,[6] was the author of numerous poems included in the imperial anthologies. When she was young she would often compose cycles of a hundred poems and write them down with ink mixed with water from the stream before these two sanctuaries; she would then offer her manuscript at the shrine. She enjoyed a truly exceptional reputation, and many of her poems were on people's lips. She was also a splendid writer of Chinese poetry and of prefaces to collections of poetry.

1. See sec. 66, n. 4.
2. Fujiwara no Sanekata (died 994) quarreled with Fujiwara no Yukinari (see above, sec. 25, n. 10). The Emperor Ichijō ordered him to go to the north; he died on his journey.
3. *Yoshimizu no kashō* was a familiar appellation of Jien (1155–1225), a high priest (*sōjō*) of Tendai Buddhism. He wrote the important historical work *Gukanshō*.
4. There is a pun on *ari* (is, or lies) and the first part of Ariwara.
5. The daughter of the Major Counselor Takatsukasa Korehira.
6. Kishi (1252–1318), the consort of the Emperor Kameyama. She took Buddhist orders in 1283.

68

There was in Tsukushi[1] a certain man, a constable of the peace[2] it would seem, who for many years had eaten two broiled radishes[3] each morning under the impression that radishes were a sovereign remedy for all ailments. Once some enemy forces attacked and surrounded his constabulary, choosing a moment when the place was deserted. Just then, two soldiers rushed out of the building, and engaged the enemy, fighting with no thought for their lives until they drove away all the enemy troops. The constable, greatly astonished, asked the two soldiers, "You have fought most gallantly, gentlemen, considering I have never seen you here before. Might I ask who you are?" "We are the radishes you have faithfully eaten every morning for so many years," they answered, and with these words they disappeared. So deep was his faith in radishes that even such a miracle could occur.

1. An old name for Kyushu.
2. An approximation of the title *ōryōshi*.
3. *Tsuchiōne* is a large variety of radish.

69

The holy man of Shosha[1] accumulated so much merit by frequent reading aloud of the Lotus Sutra that his six senses attained a state of purity. Once while on a journey, he entered an inn and heard the murmur of beans as they were boiled over a fire of bean husks. The beans were saying, "How cruel of you, who have been so close to us, to subject us to this terrible ordeal of boiling!" The husks made a crackling sound as they burnt which, the holy man could tell, meant, "Do you suppose we like doing it? Being burnt is horribly painful, but there is nothing we can do to prevent it. Don't be so angry with us."

1. Shōkū Shōnin (928–1007) lived at Mount Shosha in the province of Harima.

70

During the Gen'ō[1] era a palace concert was given in the Seisho Hall[2] just after the famous *biwa* Genjō had been lost.[3] The minister from the Chrysanthemum Pavilion[4] was to play on the *biwa* called Bokuba. He took his seat and was making sure, first of all, that the frets were in place when one fell off. He used some rice paste he kept in his wallet to fasten the fret back on the instrument. It dried satisfactorily during the presentation of the offerings to the gods, and nothing untoward occurred during the concert. A woman in the audience, who wore a silken hood, having some grievance against the musician, had sneaked up to his *biwa* and, wrenching the fret from the instrument, had replaced it as before, so that no one would detect anything was amiss.

1. The Gen'ō era lasted from 1319 to 1321; however, the event described occurred in 1318.
2. One of the nine buildings of the Buraku-in, within the palace. *Kagura* was performed here during the *Daijō-e*, the Great Thanksgiving Festival, held after the coronation of an emperor. The Emperor Go-Daigo was crowned earlier in 1318.
3. The *biwa* was stolen in 1316 and recovered in 1318.
4. Fujiwara no Kanesue (1284–1339), a famous performer on the *biwa*, was known for his love of chrysanthemums.

71

As soon as I hear a name I feel convinced I can guess what the owner looks like, but it never happens, when I actually meet the man, that his face is as I had supposed. I wonder if everybody shares my experience of feeling, when I hear some story about the past, that the house mentioned in the story must have been rather like this or that house belonging to people of today, or that the persons of the story resemble people I see now. It has happened on various occasions too that I have felt, just after someone has said something or I have seen something or thought of something, that it has occurred

[63]

before. I cannot remember *when* it was, but I feel absolutely certain that the thing has happened. Am I the only one who has such impressions?

72

Things which seem in poor taste: too many personal effects cluttering up the place where one is sitting; too many brushes in an ink-box; too many Buddhas in a family temple; too many stones and plants in a garden; too many children in a house; too many words on meeting someone; too many meritorious deeds recorded in a petition. Things which are not offensive, no matter how numerous: books in a book cart,[1] rubbish in a rubbish heap.

1. *Fuguruma* were small carts with shafts, used for moving books.

73

Is it because the truth is so boring that most stories one hears are false? People tend to exaggerate even when relating things they have actually witnessed, but when months or years have intervened, and the place is remote, they are all the more prone to invent whatever tales suit their fancies, and, when these have been written down, fictions are accepted as fact. This holds true of skill in the various arts; ignorant men who know nothing about these arts praise the masters indiscriminately, as if they were gods, but the expert gives no credence to such tales. Things known by report always prove quite different when one has actually seen them.

When a man spews forth whatever nonsense comes to his

mind, not caring that he may be exposed on the spot, people soon realize that he is lying. Again, if a man, though himself doubting the truth of a story, tells it exactly as it was related to him, with a self-satisfied twitching[1] of the nose, the lie is not *his*. But it is frightening when a man tells a lie convincingly, deliberately blurring the details in places and pretending not to remember exactly what happened, but carefully leaving no loose ends.

Nobody protests very energetically at a lie which redounds to his own prestige.

If, when everyone else is listening with pleasure to some lie, you decide that it would be pointless to be the only one to protest, "That wasn't what happened," and listen in silence, you may even be cited as a witness, and the story will seem all the more authentic.

There's no escaping it—the world is full of lies. It is safest always to accept what one hears as if it were utterly commonplace and devoid of interest.

Stories told by the lower classes are full of startling incidents. The well-bred man does not tell stories about prodigies.[2] I do not mean to suggest, however, that one should not believe wholeheartedly in the miracles of the gods and buddhas, or in the lives of the incarnations.[3] It is foolish to accept popular superstitions uncritically, but to dismiss them as being "most improbable" serves no purpose. In general, the best course is to treat such matters as if they were true, neither giving one's unqualified belief nor doubting or mocking them.[4]

1. The word *okomeku* (or *ogomeku*) has inspired much debate. One commentator devotes three closely printed pages to it. Twitching of the nose apparently indicates self-satisfaction, but some commentators believe that the man is giving the lie away by his face.

2. Reference is made to *Analects* VII, 20: "The Master never talked of prodigies, feats of strength, disorders, or spirits."
3. *Gonsha* were buddhas and bodhisattvas who temporarily assumed human form in order to save deluded human beings.
4. Kenkō recommends a suspension of disbelief with respect to such incidents as he describes in secs. 68 and 69.

74

They flock together like ants, hurry east and west, run north and south. Some are mighty, some humble. Some are aged, some young. They have places to go, houses to return to. At night they sleep, in the morning get up. But what does all this activity mean? There is no ending to their greed for long life, their grasping for profit. What expectations have they that they take such good care of themselves? All that awaits them in the end is old age and death, whose coming is swift and does not falter for one instant. What joy can there be while waiting for this end? The man who is deluded by fame and profit does not fear the approach of old age and death because he is so intoxicated by worldly cravings that he never stops to consider how near he is to his destination. The foolish man, for his part, grieves because he desires everlasting life and is ignorant of the law of universal change.

75

I wonder what feelings inspire a man to complain of "having nothing to do." I am happiest when I have nothing to distract me and I am completely alone.

If a man conforms to society, his mind will be captured

by the filth of the outside world, and he is easily led astray; if he mingles in society, he must be careful that his words do not offend others, and what he says will not at all be what he feels in his heart. He will joke with others only to quarrel with them, now resentful, now happy, his feelings in constant turmoil. Calculations of advantage will wantonly intrude, and not a moment will be free from considerations of profit and loss. Intoxication is added to delusion, and in a state of inebriation the man dreams. People are all alike: they spend their days running about frantically, oblivious to their insanity.

Even if a man has not yet discovered the path of enlightenment, as long as he removes himself from his worldly ties, leads a quiet life, and maintains his peace of mind by avoiding entanglements, he may be said to be happy, at least for the time being.

It is written in *Maka Shikan*,[1] "Break your ties with your daily activities, with personal affairs, with your arts, and with learning."

1. A basic text of Tendai Buddhism, compiled by Chang-an (561–632), the disciple of Chih-i (538–97), from his master's lectures.

76

When large numbers of people have assembled at the house of some highly esteemed family on a tragic or joyous occasion, it seems regrettable that ascetic priests[1] should mingle with the crowd, hovering at the doorway and waiting to be admitted. Even if there is some special reason for their presence, priests should keep aloof from people.

1. *Hijiri-bōshi* were mendicant priests who went from door to door, attired in rags and begging alms.

77

I find it intolerable when people who have no concern with some matter that has become a current subject of gossip acquaint themselves thoroughly with the intimate details, pass on to others their findings, or persist in further inquiries. It often happens that some country bumpkin of a priest pries into strangers' business as if it were his concern, then spreads reports so detailed it makes one wonder how he could have learned so much.

78

I find it insufferable too the way people spread word about the latest novelties and make a fuss over them. I am charmed by the man who remains unaware of such fashions until they have become quite an old story to everyone else.

The man without breeding or social graces will, when a new arrival is present, invariably mention subjects and persons familiar to the other members of a gathering, carrying on a conversation in fragments and with knowing glances and laughter, making the stranger, who fails to catch their meaning, feel like an utter ignoramus.

79

A man should avoid displaying deep familiarity with any subject. Can one imagine a well-bred man talking with the air of a know-it-all, even about a matter with which he is in fact familiar? The boor who pops up on the scene from somewhere in the hinterland answers questions with an air of utter authority in every field. As a result, though the man may also possess qualities that compel our admiration, the manner in which he displays his high opinion of himself is contemptible. It is impressive when a man is always slow to speak, even on subjects he knows thoroughly, and does not speak at all unless questioned.

80

Everybody enjoys doing something quite unrelated to his normal way of life. The priest devotes himself to the arts of the soldier; the soldier (apparently unfamiliar with the art of drawing a bow) pretends to know the Buddhist Law and amuses himself with linked verse and music. But priests and soldiers are both likely to be scorned more for these accomplishments than for their failings in their own professions.

Not only priests, but nobles, courtiers, and even men of the highest rank are often fond of arms. But though they fight a hundred times and win a hundred victories, it is no easy matter to win the reputation of a martial hero. Every man is brave when he can profit by good fortune to crush the enemy; only if a man accepts death calmly when his sword is broken and his arrows exhausted, refusing to the end to surrender, can he prove he is worthy to be called a "hero." A man has no right to boast of his martial prowess as long as he is still living. The soldier's life is remote from that of humankind and closer to that of the beasts; it is useless, unless one happens to be born into a warrior family, to indulge in the martial arts.

8 1

A screen or sliding door decorated with a painting or inscription in clumsy brushwork gives an impression less of its own ugliness than of the bad taste of the owner. It is all too apt to happen that a man's possessions betray his inferiority. I am not suggesting that a man should own nothing but masterpieces. I refer to the practice of deliberately building in a tasteless and ugly manner "to keep the house from showing its age," or adding all manner of useless things in order to create an impression of novelty, though only producing an effect of fussiness. Possessions should look old, not overly elaborate; they need not cost much, but their quality should be good.

8 2

Somebody once remarked that thin silk was not satisfactory as a scroll wrapping because it was so easily torn. Ton'a[1] replied, "It is only after the silk wrapper has frayed at top and bottom, and the mother-of-pearl has fallen from the roller that a scroll looks beautiful." This opinion demonstrated the excellent taste of the man. People often say that a set of books looks ugly if all volumes are not in the same format, but I was impressed to hear the Abbot Kōyū[2] say, "It is typical of the unintelligent man to insist on assembling complete sets of everything. Imperfect sets are better."

In everything, no matter what it may be, uniformity is undesirable. Leaving something incomplete makes it interesting, and gives one the feeling that there is room for growth.

Someone once told me, "Even when building the imperial palace, they always leave one place unfinished." In both Buddhist and Confucian writings of the philosophers of former times, there are also many missing chapters.

1. Ton'a (1289–1372) was a distinguished poet, closely associated with Kenkō, as well as a monk of the Jishū sect of Jōdo.
2. Kōyū Sōzu was a contemporary of Kenkō, but little is known about him.

83

Nothing stood in the way of the lay priest of Chikurin'in and minister of the left[1] rising to be prime minister, but he said, "I doubt that being prime minister will make much difference. I'll stop at minister of the left." He subsequently took Buddhist orders.

The Tōin minister of the left,[2] impressed by this story, himself never entertained any ambitions of becoming prime minister.

The old adage has it, "When the dragon has soared to the summit he knows the chagrin of descent." [3] The moon waxes only to wane; things reach their height only presently to decline. In all things, the principle holds true that decline threatens when further expansion is impossible.

1. Saionji Kinhira (1264–1315) became minister of the left in 1309 and took Buddhist orders in 1311.
2. Presumably Fujiwara no Saneyasu (1269–1327).
3. Derived from the I Ching (The Book of Changes).

84

When Fa-hsien[1] was in India it made him sad to see a fan from his native land, and when he lay sick he longed for

Chinese food. Someone who heard this story remarked, "To think that so eminent a man should have let people in a foreign country see how terribly weak-spirited he was!" But the Abbot Kōyū answered, "How touchingly human of him!" I felt that this comment was charming, not at all what one expects from a priest.

1. The celebrated monk (*fl.* 399–414) who spent about ten years in India and returned to China with many texts of Buddhism, which he translated from Sanskrit into Chinese.

85

Man's heart being devious, there is no absence of imposture.[1] But how could there not be a few honest men too? It commonly happens that men, though themselves not honest, are envious of the goodness they observe in others. Occasionally, it is true, some exceedingly stupid man will feel hatred for any good man he may encounter, and slander him in these terms: "That man refuses small profits because he hopes for big ones. He puts on a false front of virtue so that he may earn the reputation of being a man of integrity." The fool makes this criticism because the good man's nature differs from his own; from this it is evident that he is a man of ingrained stupidity whose nature will not change;[2] he could not even falsely refuse a small profit, nor could he even for a brief time emulate the good man.[3]

If you run through the streets, saying you imitate a lunatic, you are in fact a lunatic. If you kill a man, saying you imitate a criminal, you are a criminal yourself. By the same token, a horse that imitates a champion thoroughbred may be classed as a thoroughbred, and the man who imitates Shun[4] belongs to Shun's company. A man who studies wisdom, even insincerely, should be called wise.[5]

1. The meaning of the terms "imposture" (*itsuwari*) and "honest" (*shōjiki*) is vague. Possibly Kenkō considers as "imposters" people who pretend to wisdom they do not possess.
2. From *Analects* XVII, 3: "It is only the very wisest and the very stupidest who cannot change" (Waley's translation).
3. A curious textual variant gives *gū wo manabu bekarazu* (one should not imitate the fool) in place of *ken wo manabu bekarazu* (he could not imitate the wise man). If it is correct, there must be a break in the sentence before this statement, which logically begins the next passage. Nishio Minoru has demonstrated, however, that the older text is probably correct.
4. A legendary sage ruler of China.
5. The meaning is apparently that even going through the motions of wise or virtuous actions makes one wise or virtuous.

86

The Middle Counselor Koretsugu[1] is richly endowed as a writer of Chinese poetry. He has spent his life in Buddhist devotions and in constant reading of the sutras. Formerly, he shared quarters with Bishop En'i,[2] a priest of the Miidera, but when the temple was burned in the Bumpō era,[3] Koretsugu remarked to the bishop, "I have always called you 'priest of the temple,' but now that the temple is gone I shall call you simply 'priest.'" This was an excellent play on words.[4]

1. Taira no Koretsugu (1283–1343) became acting middle counselor on the twenty-sixth day of the second month of 1330. This passage must have been written after that date.
2. En'i Sōjō was a court poet. He is possibly the same En'i who painted the famous scroll *Ippen Shōnin Eden* in 1289.
3. The Bumpō era was 1317–19. The fire occurred in 1319.
4. The excellence of this play on words escapes most commentators.

87

One should be careful about giving drink to menials.

A man who lived in Uji had a brother-in-law in Kyoto, a hermit-priest of exquisite tastes named Gugakubō, with whom he always associated as a close friend. One day when he had sent his horse to fetch the priest, the latter said, "We have a long way ahead of us. Give the horse driver something to drink before we set out." Saké was set out before the groom, who swilled down cup after cup.

When they set out on the road the man clapped a broadsword to his side and looked so imposing that Gugakubō felt quite reassured. On the way, in the neighborhood of Kobata, they encountered some Nara priests accompanied by a large bodyguard of soldiers. The groom, accosting them, cried, "A very suspicious lot they are, here in the mountains after dark. Halt there!" He drew his sword and the others all drew theirs or fixed arrows to their bows. Gugakubō, rubbing his hands imploringly, exclaimed, "He doesn't know what he's doing —he's drunk! Please forgive him, though he doesn't deserve it." The men shouted insults at the horse-driver, but continued on their way.

The groom, turning to Gugakubō, said, "That was a mean trick to have played on me, sir. I'm not drunk. I drew my sword, hoping I might make a name for myself, but you ruined everything." In a rage, he slashed wildly at Gugakubō and cut him down. The groom then gave a great shout of "Bandits!" at which villagers swarmed out, only for him to cry, "I'm the bandit myself!" He chased after them, slashing in all directions, until finally the villagers, by force of numbers, wounded him, knocked him to the ground and tied him up.

The horse, spattered with blood, galloped back to its stable on the Uji High Road. The owner, shocked to see the rider-less horse, sent many men running off to investigate. They found Gugakubō lying prostrate and groaning in Gardenia Moor,[1] and carried him back. He barely escaped with his life, but was so badly injured by sword wounds in the back that he was left a cripple.

1. Kuchinashihara. The area of Kobata was noted for wild gardenias.

88

A certain man owned a copy of *Wakan Rōei Shū* which, he claimed, was in the hand of Ono no Tōfū.[1] Another man commented, "I am sure that there must be good reason for the attribution, sir, but does it not seem an anachronism that Tōfū should have written the manuscript of a work compiled by Fujiwara no Kintō,[2] a man born after his death? It seems rather strange." The owner replied, "That's precisely what makes this manuscript so unusual." He treasured it more than ever.

1. Ono no Tōfū (896–966) was a celebrated calligrapher.
2. Fujiwara no Kintō (966–1041), here called the Shijō major counselor, was born in the year that Ono no Tōfū died.

89

Someone remarked, "In the mountains there is a man-eating beast called the *nekomata*." [1] Another man said, "They're not only found in the mountains. Even in this neighborhood cats have grown into *nekomata,* with time and experience, and some have been known to eat people." A priest named Amidabutsu,[2] a linked-verse poet who lived near the Gyōganji,[3] heard this story and decided that he would have to be more careful henceforth when he traveled alone. Not long afterwards he was returning home alone after having spent much of the night composing linked verse at a certain place. He had reached the bank of a stream, when suddenly a *nekomata,* looking exactly as it had been described, bounded up to his feet. It leaped on the priest and tried to bite his throat. The priest was so terrified that he had not the strength to defend himself. His legs gave way and he tumbled into the river, crying, "Help! A *nekomata!* A *nekomata*'s after me!" People came running out from nearby houses with lighted torches and found the priest, a well-known figure in the neighborhood. "What happened?" they cried. When they lifted him from the river they discovered he had fallen in with the fan and little boxes won as prizes for his linked verse clutched to his bosom. Looking as if only a miracle had saved him, he crawled back into his house. Apparently his dog, recognizing its master in the dark, had jumped on him.

1. A fabulous beast, said to have eyes like a cat and the body of a dog.
2. Literally, "Something Amidabutsu." Priests at the time, particularly those belonging to the Jishū branch of the Jōdo sect, often took names ending in -amidabutsu, or -ami, for short. Such names as Kan'ami or Zeami reflect this tradition.
3. A Tendai temple in the center of Kyoto.

90

Otozurumaru, a boy in the service of the major counselor and high priest,[1] was intimate with one Sir Yasura and constantly went to visit him. Once when the boy had returned after a visit, the high priest asked him, "Where have you been?" The boy answered, "To see Sir Yasura." The boy was asked, "Is this Sir Yasura a layman or a priest?" He respectfully brought his sleeves together and replied, "I am not sure. I have never seen his head." [2] Why should he have been unable to see the man's head, I wonder.

1. This *dainagon hōin* has been identified by Tanabe Tsukasa as Ryūben (1208–83), mentioned in sec. 216 of this work.
2. If a man's head was shaven, he was a priest. The boy's ignorance suggests an indecent joke.

91

The yin-yang teachings have nothing to say on the subject of the Red Tongue Days.[1] Formerly people did not avoid these days but of late—I wonder who was responsible for starting this custom—people have taken to saying such things as "An enterprise begun on a Red Tongue Day will never see an end" or "Anything you say or do on a Red Tongue Day is bound to come to naught: you lose what you've won, your plans are undone." What nonsense! If one counted the projects begun on carefully selected "lucky days" which came to nothing in the end, there would probably be quite as many as the fruitless enterprises begun on the Red Tongue Days.

This world is a place of such uncertainty and change that what we imagine we see before our eyes really does not exist, and what has a beginning is likely to be without any end. Our aspirations are not realized, but our hopes for them never cease. We cannot be sure that the mind exists. External things are all illusions. Does anything remain unaltered even for the shortest time? Fear of Red Tongue Days comes from ignorance of these principles. It is written, "A wicked deed performed on an auspicious day will certainly prove ill-omened. A good deed performed on an unlucky day will certainly prove auspicious." Good or ill fortune is determined by man, not by the day.

1. There were five Red Tongue Days (*shakuzetsunichi*) each month. A passion for astrology in Kenkō's day made people worry about these days, which were dominated by an especially wicked demon, Rasetten.

92

A certain man who was learning to shoot a bow aimed at the target with two arrows in his hand. His teacher said, "A beginner should not hold two arrows. It will make him rely on the second arrow and be careless with the first. Each time you shoot you should think not of hitting or missing the target but of making *this* one the decisive arrow." I wonder if anyone with only two arrows would be careless with one of them in the presence of his teacher. But though the pupil is himself unaware of any carelessness, the teacher will notice it. This caution applies to all things.

A man studying some branch of learning thinks at night that he has the next day before him, and in the morning that he will have time that night; he plans in this way always to study more diligently at some future time. How much harder it is to perceive the laziness of mind that arises in an instant! Why should it be so difficult to do something now, in the present moment?

93

Someone told the story, "Let's suppose a man has an ox to sell. A buyer says he will pay the price and take the ox the following day. During the night the ox dies. The prospective buyer profits and the prospective seller loses."

A bystander, hearing the story, remarked, "The owner of the ox certainly suffered a loss, but at the same time he secured a great profit, too. You see, living creatures never realize how close they are to death. This was true of the ox, and the same is true of human beings. Unpredictably the ox died; unpredictably too the owner survived. A day of life is more precious than ten thousand pieces of gold; the worth of an ox weighs less than a duck's feather. The man who gains a fortune at the cost of a single coin cannot be said to have suffered a loss." At this everybody laughed at him. "You needn't lose an ox in order to learn the value of life," they said.

The man continued, "People who hate death should love life. How is it possible for men not to rejoice each day over the pleasure of being alive? Foolish men, forgetting this pleasure, laboriously seek others; forgetting the wealth they possess, they risk their lives in their greed for new wealth. But their desires are never satisfied. While they live they do not rejoice in life, but, when faced with death, they fear it —what could be more illogical?

"People fail to enjoy life because they do not fear death. No, it is not that they have no fear of death; rather, they forget how close it is. But if a man said he was indifferent to such external distinctions as life and death, he could certainly be said to have grasped the true principles." At this, everybody laughed at him all the more.

94

Once, when the Tokiwai prime minister[1] was on his way to the palace, he was met in the road by a warrior of the cloistered emperor's guard, who was bearing an imperial message for him. The man respectfully dismounted from his horse to present the letter. Later, the prime minister reported to the cloistered emperor, "A certain member of Your Majesty's guard dismounted for me, even though he was bearing an imperial message. How can such a man serve Your Majesty?" The man was accordingly dismissed from the guards. An imperial message should be presented while seated on horseback. The bearer should not dismount.

1. Saionji Saneuji (1194–1269), a poet and pupil of Fujiwara no Teika.

95

I once asked an expert in court usage to which loop on a box the cords should be attached. He answered, "Some say the left side, others the right. Since there is no agreement, either will do. Most document boxes have their cord attached on the right. The cord of a toilet-article box is normally attached on the left."

96

There is a plant called *menamomi*.[1] A man who has been bitten by a viper will be cured immediately if he crushes leaves from this plant and applies the crushed leaves to the wound. One must learn to recognize it.

1. Most commentators identify this plant with *yabutabako,* known by the botanical name of *carpesium abrotanoides.*

97

There are innumerable instances of things which attach themselves to something else, then waste and destroy it. The body has lice; a house has mice; a country has robbers; inferior men have riches; superior men have benevolence and righteousness; priests have the Buddhist law.[1]

1. The thought is Taoist, inspired by the passage in *Tao Te Ching*: "It was when the Great Way declined / That human kindness and morality arose" (Waley's translation). Kenkō seems to mean that superior men (*kunshi*) are so puffed up with their virtues that they become incapable of practical action, and that priests are so bound by the letter of the Buddhist law that they become inhuman.

98

These are the things I found most to my taste when I read the book called *Ichigon Hōdan*,[1] which records the sayings of the great priests:

1. When in doubt whether or not to do something, generally it is best not to do it.
2. A man concerned about the future life should not own even a *miso*[2] pot. Owning valuables, even if they happen to be personal copies of sutras or images of guardian Buddhas, is harmful to salvation.
3. The hermit's way of life is best; he feels no want even if he has nothing.
4. It is good for the man of high rank to act like a humble person, for a scholar to act like an ignoramus, for the rich man to act like a pauper, and for the talented man to act awkwardly.
5. There is only one way to seek Buddhist enlightenment: you

must lead a quiet life and pay no heed to worldly matters. This is the first essential.

There were other things, but I don't remember them.

1. A collection of Buddhist sayings relating to the Jōdo sect. The compiler and date are unknown.
2. *Miso* is a paste made of beans, commonly used in Japanese cuisine.

99

The Horikawa prime minister[1] was a handsome and affluent man who enjoyed ostentation in whatever he did. He appointed his son, Lord Mototoshi,[2] to be chief of the imperial police. When the son commenced his official functions, the father, deciding that the file chest in the office was unsightly, ordered it to be rebuilt in a more elegant style. However, this file chest had been passed down from ancient times. Nobody knew its origins, but certainly it had been there for several hundred years. This article of government property, dating back many reigns, had by its very dilapidation become a model. Officials familiar with court precedent voiced the opinion that the chest was not to be altered lightly, and Horikawa abandoned his plan.

1. Koga Mototomo (1232–97), who became prime minister in 1289.
2. Koga Mototoshi (1261–1319), who became chief of the imperial police (*kebiishi bettō*) in 1285. His father was then a major counselor, not prime minister.

100

Once, when the Koga prime minister[1] was in the palace, he wanted a drink of water. A palace servant offered him an earthenware cup. "Bring me a wooden cup,"[2] he said, and drank from it.

1. Koga Michimitsu (1187–1248).
2. *Magari* apparently meant a wooden bowl, but this is not certain. The point of the episode is that the prime minister wished to observe precedent by drinking from the correct vessel.

IOI

A certain man, who was serving as internal presiding officer at the ceremonies marking the investiture of a minister, ascended the imperial dais without first receiving the proclamation of appointment from the scribe of the secretariat. This was an unspeakable breach of etiquette, but he could not very well go back to fetch it. He was anxiously wondering what to do, when Yasutsuna,[1] the sixth-rank scribe of the prime minister, enlisted the help of a lady in a wimple, and had her carry the proclamation to the presiding officer and secretly pass it to him. He showed admirable quick-wittedness.

1. Nakahara Yasutsuna (1290–1339) was promoted in the twelfth month of 1334.

IO2

The major counselor and chief of the board of censors, the Lay Priest Mitsutada,[1] when serving as master at the Expulsion of the Demons,[2] requested instruction on the order of ceremonials from the Tōin minister of the right. The latter said, "You could not find a better teacher than that fellow Matagorō." Matagorō was an old groundsman, a man well-versed in court matters. Once when the Lord Konoe had taken his place at a ceremony, he was already summoning the secretary, having forgotten his kneeling mat, when Matagorō, who was tending the fire, whispered to him, "I think you should call for your kneeling mat first," a most amusing comment.

1. Koga Mitsutada (1284–1331).
2. See above, sec. 19, n. 10.

103

Once when the retired emperor's courtiers were playing at riddles in the Daigakuji palace,[1] the physician Tadamori[2] joined them. The Chamberlain and Major Counselor Kin'akira[3] posed the riddle: "What is it, like Tadamori, that doesn't seem to be Japanese?" Somebody gave the answer: "*Kara-heiji*—a metal wine jug."[4] The others all joined in the laugh, but Tadamori angrily stalked out.

1. Used by the Retired Sovereign Go-Uda from 1308 until his death in 1324.
2. Tamba Tadamori (fl. 1319–32) was a poet and scholar as well as a physician. His Chinese descent occasioned the witticism in this anecdote.
3. Saionji Kin'akira (1282–1336) became acting major counselor in 1336. If the text is correct, this episode must have been interpolated at a later date.
4. A complicated series of wordplays is involved. In *Heike Monogatari* the courtiers mocked Taira no Tadamori by singing about *Ise-heiji*, referring at once to the earthenware vessels (*heiji*) made in Ise, Tadamori's birthplace, and the Taira clan (*heiji*). An allusion is made here to the Chinese ancestry of another Tadamori by referring to a *Kara* (Chinese) *heiji*.

104

A certain man, thinking to call on a woman who had been living alone in dilapidated lodgings, bored with her retainers, during an enforced absence from the court, went secretly in search of her dwelling by the light of an early moon. Her dogs, suspicious of the intruder, barked furiously at him, and a scullery maid came out to demand, "Who is it, please?" The man persuaded her to admit him directly. His first glimpse of the forlorn appearance of the place made him feel sorry for the woman, and he wondered how she could endure living there. He stood for a while on the scruffy wooden floor until a waiting woman appeared and addressed him in a soft but youthful voice, "This way, please," she said. He went inside through a door that slid open reluctantly.

The interior of the house was not especially gloomy; indeed the place had charm. A lamp glowed faintly in the distance, bright enough to reveal the beauty of the furnishings, and an incense that clearly had been burning for a long time made the place seem delightful to live in.

"Make sure the gate is securely fastened. I'm afraid it may rain. Put his carriage under the gate roof, and see that his people have somewhere to rest," a voice said. Then someone whispered, "Tonight we should be able to enjoy a good night's rest." She spoke softly, so as not to be heard, but the room was so small he faintly caught her words.

Later, as the gentleman was relating in detail the many things that had happened since last they met, the first cockcrows sounded in the late night. As their intimate conversation ranged from past to future, the cockcrows, louder than before, became insistent, and he wondered if day was breaking; but as this did not seem a place where one must hurry

"A certain man, thinking to call on a woman who had been
living alone . . . went secretly in search of her dwelling . . ."

ゑつゝ宿の人々きれり

廿けつるまでもあるに

ほとく事こもり居わらと

武人とうんほえんさく

さきゞそえれつてうふ

大のちら人ーーく

夕月夜のおがつかねに

こうじきゝ

げをめの出く

てゝーりぞくへつ

やうぞ畫圖

せうめく

八ゑゝもゝ

off while the night is still dark, he tarried a bit longer. When at length the cracks in the shutters showed white, he whispered final endearments that left an unforgettable impression, and got up to depart. It was a dawn in May, when the treetops and the garden were a dazzling mass of green.

Even now he recalls the charm and loveliness of the scene, and when he passes the house he turns back to gaze at the tall bay tree until it disappears from sight.[1]

1. Kenkō attempts in this episode to evoke the atmosphere of *The Tale of Genji*, and even borrows phrases from the older work.

105

The unmelted snow lying in the shade north of the house was frozen hard, and even the shafts of a carriage drawn up there glittered with frost. The dawn moon shone clear, but its light was not penetrating. In the corridor of a deserted temple a man of obvious distinction sat beside a woman on a doorsill, chatting. Whatever it was they were discussing, there seemed no danger they would run out of things to say. The woman had a charming manner of tilting her head[1] towards the man, and I caught an occasional, enchanting whiff of some exquisite perfume. The scraps of their conversation reaching me made me long to hear the rest.

1. The words *kabushi katachi* are obscure; some scholars take them to mean "her head and features," but "tilting her head" is generally favored.

106

Once, when the holy man Shōkū of Kōya[1] was on his way to the capital, at a narrow part of the road he ran into a woman riding on a horse. Her groom failed to rein the horse, with the result that the holy man's mount was pushed into a ditch. The holy man angrily rebuked the man: "What incredible disrespect! Among the four classes of disciples of Buddha, a *bikuni* is inferior to a *biku,* an *ubasoku* to a *bikuni,* and an *ubai* to an *ubasoku.*[2] This is an unheard-of outrage—for an *ubai* like you to kick me, a *biku,* into a ditch."

The groom replied, "What do you mean, sir? I can't make sense of what you say."

The holy man, more annoyed than ever, cried, "What's that you say, you infidel, you ignoramus!" Having pronounced these harsh words, he looked as if he regretted his intemperate abuse and, turning his horse in the direction from which he had come, fled the scene. It sounds as if this was a most elevated quarrel.

1. The center of Shingon Buddhism. Nothing is known about Shōkū.
2. Gradations of Buddhist believers. A *biku* is a priest; a *bikuni,* a nun. An *ubasoku* is a male lay believer; an *ubai,* the female equivalent.

107

Few men can give a quick and apt response to a witticism from a woman, they say. During the reign of the Cloistered Emperor Kameyama[1] some mischievous court ladies made a practice of testing young men who came to court by asking if they had ever heard a nightingale sing. A certain major counselor answered, "An insignificant person the likes of myself could never be so privileged." The Horikawa minister of the interior[2] said, "I believe I have heard one at Iwakura." The women said, "That's a perfectly good answer. The major counselor's calling himself insignificant was unfortunate." Such were their evaluations.

A man should be trained in such a way that no woman will ever laugh at him. I once heard someone say that it was thanks to the instruction the Jōdōji chancellor[3] received as a boy from the Retired Empress Anki[4] that he spoke so ably. The Yamashina minister of the left[5] once said, "I feel embarrassed and nervous even when some wretched serving-girl looks at me." In a world without women it would not make any difference what kind of clothes or hat a man wore; nobody would take the trouble to dress properly.

One might wonder, then, what exalted creatures women must be to inspire such fear in men. In fact, women are all perverse by nature. They are deeply self-centered, grasping in the extreme, devoid of all susceptibility to reason, quick to indulge in superstitious practices. They are clever talkers, but may refuse to utter a word when asked even some perfectly unobjectionable question. One might suppose this meant they were cautious, but they are equally apt to start discussing, quite unsolicited, matters better passed over in silence. Their ingenuity in embroidering their stories is too much for the wisdom of any man, but when, presently, their fictions are exposed, they never perceive it. Women are devious but stupid. How disagreeable it is to be forced to cater to their wishes in order to please them. What woman is worthy of such deference? Even if such a thing as an intelligent woman existed, she would surely prove to be aloof and unendearing. Only when a man enslaved by his infatuation is courting a woman does she seem charming and amusing.

1. The Emperor Kameyama reigned from 1260 to 1272, and was a cloistered emperor (*in*) until his death in 1305.
2. Minamoto no Tomomori (1249–1316).

3. Probably Kujō Tadanori (1248–1332).
4. Fujiwara Yūshi (1207–86), the consort of the Emperor Go-Horikawa, was the aunt of Tadanori.
5. Saionji Saneo (1217–73).

108

Nobody begrudges wasting a little time. Does this represent a reasoned judgment or merely foolishness, I wonder. If I were to address myself to those who are lazy out of foolishness, I should point out that a single copper coin is of trifling value, but an accumulation of these coins will make a rich man of a poor one. That is why a merchant so jealously hoards each coin. We may not be aware of the passing instants, but as we go on ceaselessly spending them, suddenly the term of life is on us. For this reason, the man who practices the Way should not begrudge the passage of distant time to come, but the wasting of a single present moment.

If some man came and informed you that you would certainly lose your life the following day, what would you have to look forward to, what would you do to occupy yourself while waiting for this day to end? In what does the day we are now living differ from our last day? Much of our time during any day is wasted in eating and drinking, at stool, in sleeping, talking, and walking. To engage in useless activities, to talk about useless things, and to think about useless things during the brief moments of free time left us is not only to waste this time, but to blot out days that extend into months and eventually into a whole lifetime. This is most foolish of all.

Hsieh Ling-yün[1] edited the translation of the Lotus Sutra, but his mind was constantly preoccupied with his hopes for advancement; Hui-yüan[2] therefore denied him admission to the White Lotus[3] society.

A man who fails even for a short time to keep in mind the preciousness of time is no different from a corpse. If you wish to know why each instant must be guarded so jealously, it is so that a man inwardly will have no confusing thoughts and outwardly no concern with worldly matters; that if he wishes to rest at that point, he may rest, but if he wishes to follow the Way, he may follow it.

1. Hsieh Ling-yün (385–433) did not translate the Lotus Sutra but the Mahāprajñāpāramitā Sūtra, from the literal version of an interpreter. Hsieh, frustrated in his hopes for office, led a dissolute life and was finally executed.
2. A high-ranking priest (336–416) and friend of the poet T'ao Yüan-ming.
3. A society of monks and laymen headed by Hui-yüan, who set up a platform for the worship of Amida.

109

A man who was famous as a tree climber was guiding someone in climbing a tall tree. He ordered the man to cut the top branches, and, during this time, when the man seemed to be in great danger, the expert said nothing. Only when the man was coming down and had reached the height of the eaves did the expert call out, "Be careful! Watch your step coming down!" I asked him, "Why did you say that? At that height he could jump the rest of the way if he chose."

"That's the point," said the expert. "As long as the man was up at a dizzy height and the branches were threatening to break, he himself was so afraid I said nothing. Mistakes are always made when people get to the easy places."

This man belonged to the lowest class, but his words were in perfect accord with the precepts of the sages. In football too, they say that after you have kicked out of a difficult place and you think the next one will be easier you are sure to miss the ball.

110

I once asked a man rated as a champion backgammon player the secret of his success. He said, "You should never play to win, but so as not to lose. Decide which moves will lead to a quick defeat, and avoid them, choosing instead moves which seem likely to result in a slower defeat, if only by one throw of the dice."

This was the teaching of an expert in his art; the same holds true also of how a man should control his conduct or a ruler govern the state.

111

A certain priest once said that he considered it a worse offense for a man to spend his days and nights amusing himself at *go* and backgammon than to commit the Four Great Crimes[1] or the Five Capital Offenses.[2] His words still linger in my ears and seem most admirable.

1. Fornication, theft, murder, and false speech.
2. Patricide, matricide, slaying an *arhat,* bringing disharmony into Buddhist worship, or "shedding the blood of Buddha's body."

112

Would anyone ask a man who was reportedly leaving the following day for a distant country to perform some task that had to be executed slowly? A man who has urgent business to dispose of, or is afflicted by some terrible grief, has no ears for other matters, and will not ask about others' sorrows or joys. But even if he fails to make polite inquiries, nobody is resentful or asks why. The same holds true of people who have gradually become senile with age, or are beset by illness and, of course, of those who have fled the world.

Is there any of the usual social occasions which it is not difficult to avoid? But if you decide that you cannot very well ignore your worldly obligations, and that you will therefore carry them out properly, the demands on your time will multiply, bringing physical hardship and mental tension; in the end, you will spend your whole life pointlessly entangled in petty obligations.

"The day is ending, the way is long; my life already begins to stumble on its journey." [1] The time has come to abandon all ties. I shall not keep promises, nor consider decorum. Let anyone who cannot understand my feelings feel free to call me mad, let him think I am out of my senses, that I am devoid of human warmth. Abuse will not bother me; I shall not listen if praised.

1. Attributed to Po Chü-i, but not found in present editions of his works.

113

If a man over forty occasionally has a secret love affair, what can be done about it? But if he openly discusses it, or jokes about his relations with women or the private affairs of other people, it is unbecoming at his age and ugly.

In general, nothing is more unpleasant to hear or see than an old man mingling with a group of young people and relating such stories in the hope of ingratiating himself; or an undistinguished person addressing a man of reputation as if they were intimates; or a poor man, fond of feasting, going to extravagant lengths to entertain his guests.

114

Once, when the prince from Imadegawa[1] was on his way to Saga, in the neighborhood of Arisugawa, at a place where water flowed over the road, Saiōmaru[2] drove the prince's carriage oxen ahead so vigorously that water kicked up by their hooves splashed onto the front running board. Tamenori was riding escort behind the carriage. He cried, "You incredible simpleton! What do you mean by whipping the oxen in such a place?" The prince, annoyed by these words, called out, "Look, you! I'm sure you don't know as much about driving a carriage as Saiōmaru. You yourself are the incredible simpleton." He knocked Tamenori's head against the carriage.

They say that the famous Saiōmaru was the manservant of Lord Uzumasa and the keeper of the imperial carriages. The ladies who waited on Lord Uzumasa were called Hizasachi, Kototsuchi, Hōbara, and Otoushi.[3]

1. Saionji Kinsuke (1223–67).
2. A cowherd, famous in his time.
3. The names are fanciful, appropriate to cows rather than people.

"Once, when the prince from Imadegawa was on his way to
Saga . . ."

今出川のむかひ尾張駒へ

おりしけるふわらと川乃

渉うに水の源るゝ
そに

さいまち内牛を
逆つゝと枝が

あさきのろ
まりお
お板もぞ

けくやりけるを

ちちりおれ由柬の
そうれにくゝ

希め月れ童うかと
ひとそれい

もかいを
ゆき友
りくみね

115

A large number of mendicant priests had gathered at a place called Shukugawara[1] and were reciting the Invocation to the Buddha in nine stages[2] when a latecomer joined them and asked, "Excuse me, is there a priest named Irooshi among you?"

One of the number replied, "I am Irooshi. Who are you, and why do you ask?"

"My name is Shirabonji, and I have been informed that my teacher, a certain gentleman, was killed by the mendicant priest Irooshi in the Eastern Provinces, and I have come here hoping to have the honor of meeting that man and exacting vengeance. That is why I ask."

Irooshi said, "You have come on a noble mission. Yes, such a thing indeed happened. But fighting with you here would pollute this place of devotion. Let us go to the river bed before the temple and join in combat there. My fellow priests, I ask that under no circumstances you aid either of us. If this dispute should involve many, it would hinder the performance of the holy service."

The two men, having settled the circumstances of the duel, went together to the river bed where they fought to their heart's satisfaction until they ran each other through and both died.

I wonder if what we call *boroboro*—mendicant priests— actually existed in the old days. They seem to have originated in recent times under the names *boronji, bonji, kanji,* and so on. These men act as if they have abandoned the world, but have strong worldly attachments; they seem to be seeking the way of Buddha, but they make a business of quarreling. Though they are unruly and unprincipled in their behavior, their contempt for death and their utter detachment from life is appealing. I have recorded what others have told me about them.

1. Probably the place in the present Kawasaki City in Kanagawa Prefecture.
2. *Kuhon no nembutsu,* an elaborate version of the *nembutsu.*

116

The people of former times never made the least attempt to be ingenious when naming temples or other things, but bestowed quite casually whatever names suggested themselves. The names given recently sound as if they had been mulled over desperately in an attempt to display the bestower's cleverness, an unfortunate development. In giving a child a name, it is foolish to use unfamiliar characters. A craving for novelty in everything and a fondness for eccentric opinions are the marks of people of superficial knowledge.

117

Seven kinds of persons make bad friends. The first is the man of lofty position; the second, the young man; the third, the man of robust constitution who has never known a day's illness; the fourth, the man fond of liquor; the fifth, the fierce soldier; the sixth, the liar; the seventh, the miser.

Three kinds of men make desirable friends. First is the friend who gives you things; second, a doctor; and third, the friend with wisdom.

118

They say that on a day when you've eaten carp soup your sidelocks stay in place. Carp is used for making glue, no doubt because of its viscidity.

The carp is a most exalted fish, the only one which may be sliced in the presence of the emperor. Among birds, the pheasant is without peer. Pheasants and mushrooms may without objection be kept in the palace kitchen. Any other food is unseemly. The lay priest from Kitayama[1] once noticed a wild goose lying in the black-lacquered cupboard of the empress'[2] palace. When he had returned home he at once wrote her a letter saying, "I have never before seen such a creature, in its natural shape, lying in the cupboard. I am shocked. I presume this means that Your Majesty has no reliable person looking after you."

1. Saionji Sanekane (1249–1322).
2. Kishi (died 1333) was the consort of the Emperor Go-Daigo and the daughter of Sanekane.

119

The fish called *katsuo*[1] is unequaled among those caught in the sea off Kamakura, and of late has been much in demand. An old gentleman of Kamakura told me, "When we were young this fish was never served to persons of quality. Even the servants refused to eat the head. They cut it off and threw it away." It is typical of these degenerate times that such fish have become accepted by the upper classes.

1. *Katsuo* is the bonito.

120

Even if we were deprived of Chinese goods, we should not miss them, except for medicines. Many Chinese books are available all over the country, and anyone who wishes can copy one. It is the height of foolishness that Chinese ships should make the dangerous journey over here, crammed with cargoes of useless things.

I believe it is written in the classics somewhere, "He did not prize things from afar," [1] and again, "He did not value treasures that were hard to obtain." [2]

1. From *Shu Ching* (*The Book of History*).
2. From *Tao Te Ching*: "Therefore the Sage wants only things that are unwanted, / Sets no store by products difficult to get" (Waley).

121

Domestic animals include the horse and the ox. It is a pity we must bind and afflict them, but unavoidable, since they are indispensable to us. You should certainly keep a dog; dogs are better than men at watching and protecting a house. However, every house already has a dog anyway, so you need not search for one especially for this purpose.

All other birds and beasts are useless. When animals that run are confined to pens or fastened with chains, when birds that fly have their wings clipped or are put in cages, the longing of the birds for the clouds and the grief of the animals over separation from their mountains will be unceasing. How can any man who is capable of imagining how wretched he would feel under the circumstances take pleasure in keeping these pets? A man who enjoys torturing living creatures is

"Domestic animals . . ."

風をひく物は
馬牛ほなど
つくつくなど
さてゐるねわざれ
ゐ
大い
まわりうせぐ
つまめ
人々も
ゆさりくれが
くくど
カゝド
いぞいきん

of the same company as Chieh and Chou.[1] Wang Tzu-yu[2] loved birds, but for him this meant watching them sport in the woods and making them the companions of his walks. He did not catch and torture them.

It is stated in the classics, "Rare birds and strange beasts should not be kept in this country."[3]

1. Two legendary emperors of China, known for their extreme cruelty. Chieh was the last of the Hsia dynasty, Chou the last of the Shang dynasty.
2. Also known as Wang Hui-tzu, a fourth-century calligrapher and man of elegance.
3. From *Shu Ching*.

122

The most important qualifications of a man are familiarity with the classics and a knowledge of the teachings of the sages. Next is handwriting; even if a man does not make this art his chief study, he should learn it anyway, for it will help him in his learning. Next, he should study medicine. A knowledge of medicine is indispensable in order to keep oneself in good health, to help others, and to fulfil one's duties of loyalty and filial affection. Next, archery and riding certainly deserve attention, for they are listed among the Six Arts.[1] A knowledge of letters, arms, and medicine is truly essential. Any man who would study these arts cannot be called an idler.

Next, since food nurtures man like Heaven itself, a knowledge of how to prepare tasty food must be accounted a great asset in a man. Next comes manual skill, which has innumerable uses.

As for other things, too many accomplishments are an embarrassment to the gentleman.[2] Proficiency in poetry and music, both noble arts, has always been esteemed by rulers and subjects alike, but it would seem that nowadays they are neglected as a means of governing the country. Gold is the finest of the metals but it cannot compare to iron in its many uses.

1. The Six Arts were rites, music, archery, riding, calligraphy, and mathemathics.
2. A reference to *Analects* IX, 6: "Does it befit a gentleman to have many accomplishments? No, he is in no need of them at all" (Waley).

123

A man who wastes his time doing useless things is either a fool or a knave. Many things must be done, like it or not, for your country or lord, and they leave you little time of your own. Consider: for his own welfare a man has no choice but to labor so he may secure food, clothing, and shelter. Man's worldly necessities do not go beyond these three. When he can live peacefully, neither hungry nor cold nor buffeted by the wind and rain, he is happy. But all men are prey to sickness, and when sickness strikes, the pains are hard to bear; the healing art should not be forgotten. Adding medicine gives four essentials. If a man needs but cannot obtain them, he is poor; if he lacks none of the four, he is rich. If one seeks to obtain more than these four, it is extravagance. Why should anyone who is modest in his demands for these four ever feel that he has not enough?

124

The priest Zehō[1] ranks second to none as a scholar of the Pure Land Sect, but instead of making a show of his learning, he recites the *nembutsu* day and night, a quiet way of life that I find most admirable.

1. A poet and contemporary of Kenkō's.

125

For the Buddhist services on the forty-ninth day after a man's death, the family summoned a certain holy man who preached so beautifully that everybody wept. After he had left, those who had heard the sermon remarked to one another in admiration that the services that day had been more inspiring than usual. Somebody countered, "It is not surprising, when you consider how much he looks like a Chinese dog." [1] At these words the atmosphere of awe dissolved, and everybody was amused. Who ever heard of praising a priest in such terms?

Again, I heard it remarked that if, when offering saké to someone, you first drink some yourself and then try to force it on the other man, it is like trying to kill a man with a double-edged sword; since the blade cuts both ways, you are likely in lifting it to cut your own throat before you can cut the other man's. If you are the first to fall into a drunken stupor, no one else is likely to drink. I wonder if the man who made these remarks had ever tried to kill anyone with a double-edged sword. It was really amusing.

1. The implications of the remark are not clear. Perhaps reference is being made to *koma-inu*, the stone dog before a Shinto shrine.

126

Someone once told me, "When a man has been losing heavily at gambling and then declares his intention of betting all the money he has left, you should not gamble with him. You should recognize that the time has come for his luck to turn and for him to start a winning streak. A good gambler knows when that time has come."

127

It is best not to change something if changing it will not do any good.

128

The Major Counselor Masafusa[1] was a learned and virtuous man. The cloistered emperor[2] was thinking of making him general of the inner palace guards when a man in personal attendance reported to him, "I have just seen a most horrible sight." "What was it?" His Majesty asked. The man replied, "Through a hole in the fence between his house and mine I saw Lord Masafusa cut off the legs of a living dog to feed to his hawks." The emperor, hearing this, decided that Masafusa must be a vile and loathsome man. His customary partiality towards Masafusa gave way to estrangement, and he did not promote him. It was odd that such a man should keep hawks, but the story about the dog's legs was completely untrue. Masafusa was the unfortunate victim of the lie, but the emperor's feelings of revulsion when he heard the story bespeak his nobility.

As a rule, people who take pleasure in killing living creatures or making one creature fight another, are themselves akin to the beasts of prey. If we carefully observe the countless varieties of birds and beasts, even tiny insects, we shall discover that they love their children, long to be near their parents, that husband and wife remain together, that they are jealous, angry, greedy, self-seeking, and fearful for their own lives to an even worse degree than men because they lack intelligence. How can we not feel pity when pain is inflicted on them or people take their lives?

A man who can look on sentient creatures without feeling compassion is no human being.

1. Minamoto no Masafusa (1261–1302).
2. Probably the Emperor Go-Uda (reigned 1274–87), but possibly the Emperor Go-Fushimi (reigned 1298–1301).

129

Yen Hui said that his desire in life was never to cause other people any trouble.[1] Obviously, it is wrong to make others suffer, to torture living creatures, or to force even the humblest person to do anything against his will.[2] Some take pleasure in deceiving or frightening or humiliating innocent children. The adult may think nothing of this, since he does it in jest, but the child will experience truly intense feelings of heartrending fear, shame, and rejection. Anyone who enjoys bringing distress to a child lacks all feelings of humanity.

Joy, anger, grief, or pleasure, as experienced by adults,

are all empty delusions, but who does not give himself to them as if they were real? It harms a man far more to wound his spirit than to break his body. Diseases too are caught mainly through the mind. Few diseases originate without. Sometimes it happens that medicine taken to induce perspiration has no effect, but a man invariably sweats when he is ashamed or afraid, a sign of what the mind can do. The man who inscribed the plaque on the Ling-yün tower turned white-haired with fright,[3] and there is no dearth of similar examples.

1. From *Analects* V, 25: "Yen Hui said, 'I should never like to boast of my good qualities nor make a fuss about the trouble I take on behalf of others'" (Waley).
2. From *Analects* IX, 25: "You may rob the Three Armies of their commander-in-chief, but you cannot deprive the humblest person of his opinion" (Waley). In both this quotation and the previous one Kenkō has altered the meaning of the original text.
3. A reference to the story of Wei Tan, a calligrapher of the Wei Dynasty (220–65), who was lifted in a basket to a height of 250 feet so that he might inscribe the plaque. His hair was white by the time he returned to the ground. Kenkō probably learned the story from a Japanese work like *Jikkunshō*, compiled in 1256.

130

Avoid contention with others, bend yourself to their views, put yourself last and other people first—that is the best course.

People enjoy competition in games because they like to win. They rejoice that their skill is greater than anybody else's. Obviously, then, they will find it unpleasant to lose. If you deliberately let yourself be beaten in the hope of pleasing your opponent, you will certainly derive no pleasure from the game yourself. On the other hand, it goes against all decency to enjoy the humiliation of others.

Even when amusing themselves with their dearest friends, people enjoy the feeling of superior intelligence that comes from tricking and duping them. This too is contrary to proper behavior. Often what has started as a friendly diversion at a party develops into protracted enmity. Such are the unfortunate consequences of a love of competition.

If you wish to be superior to others, you had best devote yourself to your studies and trust that the knowledge you gain will exceed theirs; if you pursue learning you will know better than to take pride in your wisdom or to compete with your friends. Only the strength that comes with learning can enable a man to refuse high office and reject material gain.

131

The poor man supposes that courtesy involves giving presents; the aged man, that courtesy consists in expending one's energy. True wisdom consists in knowing your own capacity and stopping at once when something is too much for you. If the other person refuses to let you stop, that is his fault. If you are ignorant of your own capacity and exert yourself beyond your strength, that is your mistake.

A poor man who does not know his own capacity will steal; a man whose strength has failed, but who does not know it, will fall sick.

132

The Toba New Road did not acquire its name after the Toba Palace[1] was built. The name is an old one. It is recorded, I understand, in the diary of Prince Rihō[2] that when Prince Motoyoshi[3] recited congratulations to the throne on New Year's morning, his voice was so powerful that it could be heard from the imperial council hall all the way to the Toba New Road.

1. Built by the Emperor Shirakawa in 1086 and enlarged by the Emperor Toba. It was at Toba, south of Kyoto.
2. Another name for Prince Shigeaki (906–54), a son of the Emperor Daigo. This item is not found in surviving portions of his diary.
3. Prince Motoyoshi (890–943), the eldest son of the Emperor Yōzei.

133

The pillow in the emperor's bedchamber is placed to the east. Sleeping with one's pillow to the east enables one, as a rule, to come under the influence of the yang principle: that is why Confucius also slept with his head to the east. Bedchambers are usually constructed in such a way that sleeping with a pillow to the south is also common. The Cloistered Emperor Shirakawa slept with his head to the north.[1] The north, however, is to be avoided. Someone also commented, "Ise lies to the south. Do you think it was proper for an emperor to sleep with his feet towards the great shrine?" However, when the emperor worships the great shrine from afar, he faces southeast and not south.

1. Sleeping with one's head to the north and lying on the right side would be in imitation of Buddha's posture as he prepared to enter Nirvana.

134

A certain ascetic priest, a *samadhi*[1] monk of the Hokke Hall at the tomb of the Cloistered Emperor Takakura,[2] once took a mirror and carefully examined his face. He was so depressed by its ugliness and meanness that he felt a loathing even for the mirror. For a long time afterwards he was too afraid of mirrors even to take one in his hands, and he gave up all intercourse with people. He appeared only for services at the hall, and otherwise remained in seclusion. This story struck me as being most noteworthy.

Even people who seem quite intelligent make judgments entirely on the basis of what they observe of other people, and know nothing about themselves. But surely it is illogical to know others and not oneself. A man who knows himself deserves to be called a learned man.

A man may not realize it though he is ugly, foolish, inept at his profession, of no consequence in the world, old, ravaged by sickness, close to death, unable to attain the Way of Buddha despite his prayers; ignorant of his own failings, he is still less aware of the criticisms others direct at him. But a man can see his face in the mirror and he can tell his age by counting. It is by no means impossible to know oneself. But, some may argue, unless one can do something about it, it is just the same as not knowing oneself.

I am not suggesting that anyone should change his face or become younger. What I am saying is: if you know you are no good at your profession, why not retire at once? If you know you are old, why not live in some quiet retreat, taking good care of yourself? If you know that your devotions are inadequate, why not give yourself to them completely?

To mix in company where you are not welcome is shaming. If, though you are ugly and slow-witted, you persist in serving at court; if, though you are badly educated, you associate with great scholars; if, though you have no artistic talent yourself, you mingle with accomplished artists; if, with the snow of age on your head, you take your place beside a man in the pride of his youth; and if, especially, you hope for what you cannot achieve, fret over schemes beyond your capacity, wait for things that will not come, fearing and flattering others, the shame you incur will not have been imposed by others; it is a disgrace you will have brought upon yourself by your own greed. Our greed is unceasing because we are never sure that the great event that ends our life has come and is here now before us.

1. *Sammai-sō* were Tendai monks who gained *samadhi* through contemplation of the Lotus Sutra.
2. The tomb of Takakura is near Seikanji, a temple east of Kyoto.

135

The man known as Sukesue,[1] the major counselor and lay priest, said on meeting Tomouji,[2] the middle captain of the chancellor, "Any question you could possibly ask me, I am sure I can answer." "I'm not so sure," said Tomouji. "Well, then," said Sukesue, "test me." "I've never studied any proper book learning, so I can't ask about that. I'll ask you instead, if I may, about something of no importance that's been puzzling me." "If it's some trivial thing from daily life, I'm all the more certain I can explain it, whatever it may be," said Sukesue. The courtiers and ladies in waiting cried, "What an amusing dispute! If it's all the same to you, why not have it out before His Majesty? The one who loses will provide a feast." They agreed to follow this suggestion, and were summoned before His Majesty to have their dispute. Tomouji asked, "There is an expression I have heard ever since I was a boy, but I don't know what it means. What do they mean when they say, *'Uma no kitsuryō, kitsuni no oka, naka kubore iri kurendō'?* [3] That's my question for you." Sukesue was at a loss for an answer. "This is nonsense. It is not worth explaining," he said. Tomouji replied, "I told you from the start that I didn't know anything about deep matters. We agreed that I would ask you something nonsensical." The major counselor and lay priest, beaten in the dispute, was obliged to offer a splendid feast as a penalty, I am told.

1. Fujiwara no Sukesue (1207–89), respected in his day both as a poet and an authority on court usages.
2. Minamoto no Tomouji (1273–75).
3. Scholars have puzzled over this riddle (if that is what it is) for centuries, but no convincing explanation has been offered.

136

The physician Atsushige was in attendance on the late cloistered emperor[1] when His Majesty's dinner was served. He said, "If Your Majesty will deign to ask me to write the names and properties of each of the dishes which have now been brought before you, I shall answer you from memory. Then I should like Your Majesty to compare what I say with a book of natural science.[2] I am confident that I shall not make a single mistake." Just at this moment Arifusa, the late minister of the interior of Rokujō,[3] entered. "This is a fine opportunity to learn something myself," he said. "First of all, with which radical do you write the character *shio,* for salt?" "With the earth radical,"[4] answered Atsushige. "It's quite apparent already how learned you are. That will be enough for now. I have nothing else to ask." Everyone laughed heartily and Atsushige withdrew.

1. The Emperor Go-Uda, who died in 1324.
2. *Honsō* was primarily the study of medicinal herbs, but included also zoology and mineralogy.
3. Minamoto no Arifusa (1251–1319), a poet and critic of poetry.
4. The character is today normally written with an abbreviation using this radical, but this was formerly considered vulgar; the "correct" character is highly complicated.

137

Are we to look at cherry blossoms only in full bloom, the moon only when it is cloudless? To long for the moon while looking on the rain, to lower the blinds and be unaware of the passing of the spring—these are even more deeply moving. Branches about to blossom or gardens strewn with faded flowers are worthier of our admiration. Are poems written on such themes as "Going to view the cherry blossoms only to find they had scattered" or "On being prevented from visiting the blossoms" inferior to those on "Seeing the blossoms"? People commonly regret that the cherry blossoms scatter or that the moon sinks in the sky, and this is natural; but only an exceptionally insensitive man would say, "This branch and that branch have lost their blossoms. There is nothing worth seeing now."

In all things, it is the beginnings and ends that are interesting. Does the love between men and women refer only to the moments when they are in each other's arms? The

"Are we to look at cherry blossoms only in full bloom, the moon
only when it is cloudless?   .   .   .   It is the rustic boors who take all
their pleasures grossly . . ."

man who grieves over a love affair broken off before it was fulfilled, who bewails empty vows, who spends long autumn nights alone, who lets his thoughts wander to distant skies, who yearns for the past in a dilapidated house—such a man truly knows what love means.

The moon that appears close to dawn after we have long waited for it moves us more profoundly than the full moon shining cloudless over a thousand leagues. And how incomparably lovely is the moon, almost greenish in its light, when seen through the tops of the cedars deep in the mountains, or when it hides for a moment behind clustering clouds during a sudden shower! The sparkle on hickory or white-oak leaves seemingly wet with moonlight strikes one to the heart. One suddenly misses the capital, longing for a friend who could share the moment.

And are we to look at the moon and the cherry blossoms with our eyes alone? How much more evocative and pleasing it is to think about the spring without stirring from the house, to dream of the moonlit night though we remain in our room!

The man of breeding never appears to abandon himself completely to his pleasures; even his manner of enjoyment is detached. It is the rustic boors who take all their pleasures grossly. They squirm their way through the crowd to get under the trees; they stare at the blossoms with eyes for nothing else; they drink saké and compose linked verse; and finally they heartlessly break off great branches and cart them away. When they see a spring they dip their hands and feet to cool them; if it is the snow, they jump down to leave their footprints. No matter what the sight, they are never content merely with looking at it.

Such people have a very peculiar manner of watching the

Kamo Festival. "The procession's awfully late," they say. "There's no point waiting in the stands for it to come." They go off then to a shack behind the stands where they drink and eat, play *go* or backgammon, leaving somebody in the stands to warn them. When he cries, "It's passing now!" each of them dashes out in wild consternation, struggling to be first back into the stands. They all but fall from their perches as they push out the blinds and press against one another for a better look, staring at the scene, determined not to miss a thing. They comment on everything that goes by, with cries of "Look at this! Look at that!" When the procession has passed, they scramble down, saying, "We'll be back for the next one." All they are interested in is what they can see.

People from the capital, the better sort, doze during the processions, hardly looking at all. Young underlings are constantly moving about, performing their masters' errands, and persons in attendance, seated behind, never stretch forward in an unseemly manner. No one is intent on seeing the procession at all costs.

It is charming on the day of the Festival to see garlands of hollyhock leaves carelessly strewn over everything. The morning of the Festival, before dawn breaks, you wonder who the owners are of the carriages silently drawn up in place, and guess, "That one is his—or his," and have your guesses confirmed when sometimes you recognize a coachman or servant. I never weary of watching the different carriages going back and forth, some delightfully unpretentious, others magnificent. By the time it is growing dark you wonder where the rows of carriages and the dense crowds of spectators have disappeared to. Before you know it, hardly a soul is left, and the congestion of returning carriages is over. Then they start removing the blinds and matting from the stands, and the place, even as you watch, begins to look desolate. You realize with a pang of grief that life is like this. If you have seen the avenues of the city, you have seen the festival.

I suddenly realized, from the large number of people I could recognize in the crowds passing to and fro before the stands, that there were not so many people in the world, after all. Even if I were not to die until all of them had gone, I should not have long to wait. If you pierce a tiny aperture in a large vessel filled with water, even though only a small amount drips out, the constant leakage will empty the vessel. In this capital, with all its many people, surely a day never passes without someone dying. And are there merely one or two deaths a day? On some days, certainly, many more than one or two are seen to their graves at Toribeno, Funaoka, and other mountainsides, but never a day passes without a single funeral. That is why coffin makers never have any to spare. It does not matter how young or how strong you may be, the hour of death comes sooner than you expect. It is an extraordinary miracle that you should have escaped to this day; do you suppose you have even the briefest respite in which to relax?

When you make a *mamagodate*[1] with backgammon counters, at first you cannot tell which of the stones arranged before you will be taken away. Your count then falls on a certain stone and you remove it. The others seem to have escaped, but as you renew the count you will thin out the pieces one by one, until none is left. Death is like that. The soldier who goes to war, knowing how close he is to death, forgets his family and even forgets himself; the man who has turned his back on the world and lives in a thatched hut, quietly taking pleasure in the streams and rocks of his garden, may suppose that death in battle has nothing to do with him, but this is a shallow misconception. Does he imagine that, if he hides in the still recesses of the mountains, the enemy called change will fail to attack? When you confront death, no matter where it may be, it is the same as charging into battle.

1. A kind of mathematical puzzle. Fifteen white and fifteen black stones are so arranged that eliminating the tenth stone, counting in one direction, will result after fourteen rounds in only one white stone remaining. If the count is then resumed in the opposite direction, all the black stones will be eliminated, leaving the one white stone. The game was known in Europe too, and credited to Josephus. The Japanese name *mamagodate* (stepchild disposition) derives from the story of a man with fifteen children by one wife and fifteen by another; his estate was disposed of by means of the game, one stepchild in the end inheriting all.

138

Once, after the Festival had ended, a certain person had all the hollyhock leaves removed from his blinds, with the remark that they were no longer of any use. I felt that this showed a want of taste, but since he was a person of quality, I supposed he must have his reasons. But there is a poem by Lady Suō:[1]

kakuredomo	Though still they hang,
kai naki mono wa	They serve no purpose now,
morotomo ni	Those withering leaves
misu no aoi no	Of hollyhocks, left on the blinds,
kareba narikeri	We cannot see together.[2]

This poem, in her *Collected Works,* refers to the withered

hollyhock leaves hung on the bamboo blinds of a palace room. The prose prefaces to old poems sometimes also say, "Sent attached to some withered hollyhocks." The *Pillow Book* contains the passage, "Things which arouse nostalgia for the past—withered hollyhocks." This seems to me a wonderfully evocative observation. In the *Tales of the Four Seasons*[3] by Kamo no Chōmei, he too says, "The hollyhocks after the Festival still cling to the palace blinds." How could anyone have removed all the leaves, when it is sad enough that they should wither of themselves?

The medicinal sachets hung round the curtained dais in a nobleman's chamber are replaced on the ninth day of the ninth month with chrysanthemums, evidence that irises should be left until chrysanthemum time. After the Dowager Empress of the Apricot Palace[4] had passed away, Ben no Menoto,[5] discovering withered irises and medicinal sachets inside an old, curtained bedstead, wrote the lines, "I hang up unseasonable roots, lifting my wailing voice." In reply, Gō Jijū[6] composed the poem, "Though the iris stalks remain, did ever I think I should see her bedchamber so desolate?"

1. Identified by most commentators as the daughter of Taira no Tsugunaka, governor of Suō. Many poems by Lady Suō were included in court anthologies.
2. The poem is studded with puns, including: *misu* (blinds) and *mizu* (not seeing); *aoi* (hollyhock) and *au hi* (day of meeting); *kare* (separation) and *kareba* (withered leaves).
3. *Shiki no Monogatari* is no longer credited to Kamo no Chōmei.
4. Fujiwara Kenshi (994–1027), the daughter of Fujiwara no Michinaga, who became the consort of the Emperor Sanjō.
5. Daughter of Fujiwara no Masatoki and nurse to Kenshi's daughter. Thirty of Ben no Menoto's poems may be found in court anthologies. The poem quoted here is found in full in *Senzaishū* (1188).
6. Gō Jijū was the daughter of Ōe Masahira (952–1012) and Lady Akazome-emon. This poem is included in *Senzaishū*.

139

The trees I should like for my house are pine and cherry. Five-needled pines will do. As for cherry blossoms, the single-petaled variety is preferable. The double-cherry trees formerly grew only at the capital in Nara, but lately they seem to have become common everywhere. The cherry blossoms of Yoshino and the "left guard" tree[1] of the palace are all single. The double-petaled cherry is an oddity, most exaggerated and perverse. One can do quite nicely without planting it. The late-blooming cherry is also unattractive, and even disagreeable when infested by caterpillars. In plum blossoms I prefer the white and the pink. The early-blossoming single variety and the charmingly scented double crimson are both agreeable. The late plum, flowering in competition with the cherry, suffers by contrast; indeed, it is overwhelmed. It is unpleasant, moreover, to see the withered blossoms clinging to the boughs. The Kyōgoku middle counselor and lay priest[2] planted single plum trees near his eaves, saying how impetuous and charming the plum blossoms must be to flower and scatter before any others. Two of these plum trees apparently still survive on the south side of his house in Kyōgoku. Willows are also charming. Young maple leaves about the beginning of the fourth month are lovelier than any flowers or autumn leaves. Orange trees and laurels both look best when the trunks are old and big.

Among plants the best are kerria roses, wisteria, irises, and pinks. For a pond, water lilies are best. Among autumn plants I prefer reeds, pampas grass, bellflowers, *hagi, ominaeshi, fujibakama,* asters, burnet, *karukaya,* gentians, and chrysanthemums.[3] Yellow chrysanthemums are also good.

"The trees I should like for my house are pine and cherry . . ."

家つくりそれ木いれ梅
れ〳〵又もろ〳〵れいさ〳〵
なりらう〳〵ハ年ほこ〳〵うの
初のミもかけるをじころそ
せにゆハくゆろ〳〵なりも吉丹
乃花右迫のさくらかた〳〵く
〳〵こゑあれ〳〵八年ほ〳〵う〳〵い
さ〳〵ゆうのわたりゆ〳〵ふらく
れぢあらう〳〵どともあるを
ん おそさく〳〵みとこ〳〵ゆ
生の行〳〵も〳〵つう〳〵
柳〳〵ねり〳〵卯月
こうられみるえで
すづく〳〵ろげれ花
りみろみもまふり

Ivy, arrowroot vine, and morning glories are all best when they grow on a low fence, not too high nor too profusely. It is hard to feel affection for other plants—those rarely encountered, or which have unpleasant-sounding Chinese names, or which look peculiar. As a rule, oddities and rarities are enjoyed by persons of no breeding. It is best to be without them.

1. The *sakon no sakura,* planted to the east of the steps leading down into the courtyard south of the ceremonial palace (*shishinden*). An orange tree (*tachibana*) was planted west of the steps.
2. Fujiwara no Teika (1162–1241), the great poet and critic.
3. The botanical names of these plants are as disagreeable to our ears as Kenkō found Chinese names. *Hagi* is lespedeza; *ominaeshi* is *patrinia scabiosaefolia*; *fujibakama* is agrimony; and *karukaya* is *anthistiria arguens.*

140

The intelligent man, when he dies, leaves no possessions. If he has collected worthless objects, it is embarrassing to have them discovered. If the objects are of good quality, they will depress his heirs at the thought of how attached he must have been to them. It is all the more deplorable if the possessions are ornate and numerous. If a man leaves possessions, there are sure to be people who will quarrel disgracefully over them, crying, "*I'm* getting that one!" If you wish something to go to someone after you are dead, you should give it to him while you are still alive. Some things are probably indispensable to daily life, but as for the rest, it is best not to own anything at all.

141

The holy man Gyōren of the Hiden-in,[1] whose lay name was Miura, was an incomparable soldier.

Once a man from his native place came and, in the course of the conversation, remarked, "You can trust what a man from the east says. People from the capital are good at making promises, but they're not to be trusted."

The holy man answered, "I can see why you might think so, but having lived in the capital for a long time and become thoroughly acquainted with the people, I don't think they are any worse by nature. They are so gentle and warm-hearted that they cannot bear to refuse outright whatever anyone may ask of them. Because they are incapable of speaking out their thoughts, they consent helplessly to every request. It is not that they intentionally deceive others, but most of them are poor and cannot do as they would like. It often happens then, quite predictably, that they fail to carry out their promises. People from the east, though I am one of them myself, lack such gentleness in their hearts or sympathy for others. They are brusque through and through, and say 'No' from the start so as to discourage requests. Their prosperity makes people trust them."

Such was his explanation. This holy man spoke with a provincial accent. His voice was harsh and I doubt that he had much understanding of the fine points of the sacred teachings. But this one utterance attracted me to him, and I felt that his having been chosen from among many priests as abbot of the temple must have been due to this warm side of his nature, and that this quality was sufficient recommendation for the man.

1. Nothing is known about Gyōren Shōnin. The Hiden-in, situated in the north of Kyoto, was a temple where the sick were treated and orphans lodged.

142

Even a man who seems devoid of intelligence occasionally says an apt word. A fierce-looking brute of a soldier once asked a companion, "Have you got any kids?" "Not one," replied the other. "Then," said the soldier, "I don't suppose you know what deep feelings are. You probably haven't a drop of human warmth in you. That's a frightening thought! It's having children that makes people understand the beauty of life." He was right. Would any tenderness of feeling exist in such a man's heart if not for the natural affection between parent and child? Even the man with no sense of duty towards his parents learns what parental solicitude means when he has a child of his own.

It is wrong for anyone who has abandoned the world and is without attachments to despise other men burdened with many encumbrances for their deep-seated greed and constant fawning on others. If he could put himself in the place of the men he despises, he would see that, for the sake of their parents, wives, and children, whom they truly love, they forget all sense of shame and will even steal. I believe therefore that it would be better, instead of imprisoning thieves and concerning ourselves only with punishing crimes, to run the country in such a way that no man would ever be hungry or cold. When a man lacks steady employment, his heart is not steady, and in extremity he will steal. As long as the country is not properly governed and people suffer from cold and hunger, there will never be an end to crime. It is pitiful to make people suffer, to force them to break the law, and then to punish them.

How then may we help the people? If those at the top would give up their luxury and wastefulness, protect the people, and encourage agriculture, those below would unquestionably benefit greatly. The real criminal is the man who commits a crime even though he has a normal share of food and clothing.

143

When I hear people say that a man's last hours were splendid, I always think how impressive it would be if they meant merely that his end was peaceful and free of agony; but foolish people embellish the story with strange and unusual details, singling out for praise words that he said or things that he did which suit their own preferences, but which hardly accord with the man's usual behavior.

This great occasion is not to be evaluated even by an incarnation of the Buddha,[1] nor can learned doctors judge it. As long as a man does nothing unseemly at the hour of his death, nothing people may have seen or heard is of significance.

1. This statement has been variously interpreted: not even incarnations of the Buddha nor learned doctors can foretell the manner of their own deaths; not even incarnations or learned doctors can guess what another man experiences during his last moments; outsiders cannot predict the manner of death even of incarnations and learned doctors. The Japanese language is vague enough to permit three such divergent interpretations.

144

Once, when the holy man of Toganoo[1] was journeying along a road he encountered a man washing a horse by a river. *"Ashi, ashi,"* [2] said the man. The holy man stopped in his tracks and exclaimed, "How inspiring! Some deed of virtue in a previous existence has brought this man enlightenment! He is reciting the invocation *aji, aji!* [3] I wonder whose horse it might be? Such piety overcomes me." When he asked about the owner, the man replied, "The horse belongs to Lord Fushō." "Splendid!" cried the holy man. "This is truly a case of *aji hon fushō.*[4] What a fortunate link you have established with the Way of the Buddha!" He wiped away the tears of gratitude.

1. Myōe Shōnin (1172–1232), who founded Kōzanji, a temple west of Kyoto.
2. *Ashi* means "leg." The man was telling the horse to lift its leg.
3. The holy man mistakenly supposes the man is saying *aji,* the first letter of the Sanskrit alphabet, used in Shingon ritual.
4. The formula *aji hon fushō* means that there is no beginning of creation; that is, the world has always existed. The combination of the man's cry of *aji* and the name Fushō delights the holy man, who remembers the formula.

145

The imperial bodyguard Hata no Shigemi once said of Shingan, the lay prince of Shimotsuke, a member of the retired emperor's guard, "His face has the marks of a man who will fall from his horse. You should urge him to be careful." Nobody took his words seriously, but Shingan one day fell from his horse and died. People were then convinced that the opinions of anyone expert in this art were to be trusted like divine pronouncements. They asked Shigemi what signs enabled him to make the prediction. He said, "Shingan sat unsteadily in the saddle and liked high-spirited horses. Those were the signs he carried. When have I ever been mistaken in a prediction?"

146

Myōun,[1] the abbot of the Enryakuji, once asked a physiognomist, "Am I in any danger from weapons?" The man said, "Indeed, the sign is in your face." "What kind of sign is it?" asked Myōun. The man replied, "A person in your position should be in no danger of a violent death, but the very fact that you thought of such a thing and asked me, however lightly, is in itself a portent of danger." As a matter of fact, the abbot was killed by an arrow.

1. Myōun Zasu (1115–83) was killed by a stray arrow during the revolt of Minamoto no Yoshinaka.

147

Of late people have begun to say that a great many scars from moxa treatment[1] render a man unclean for performing the sacred rites. Nothing to that effect is found in the ancient regulations.

1. Burning of an herb (*mogusa*) at prescribed points on the skin.

"Of late people have begun to say that a great many scars from moxa treatment . . . A man over forty who takes moxa treatment . . ."

炎暑のあまさくにてり
ねばる里
れば涼味に
けがれなく、二
らくの
ひ出てる
みを
格式きて
ねらど
みそぐぞ

148

A man over forty who takes moxa treatment but does not have moxa burnt on his kneecaps may have dizzy spells. He should by all means have it burnt in those places.

149

You should never put the new antlers of a deer to your nose and smell them. They have little insects that crawl into the nose and devour the brain.

150

A man who is trying to learn some art is apt to say, "I won't rush things and tell people I am practicing while I am still a beginner. I'll study by myself, and only when I have mastered the art will I perform before people. How impressed they'll be then!"

People who speak in this fashion will never learn any art. The man who, even while still a novice, mixes with the experts, not ashamed of their harsh comments or ridicule, and who devotedly persists at his practice, unruffled by criticism, will neither become stultified in his art nor careless with it. Though he may lack natural gifts, he will with the passage of the years outstrip the man who coasts on his endowments, and in the end will attain the highest degree of skill, acquire authority in his art and the recognition of the public, and win an unequaled reputation.

The performers who now rank as the most skilled in the whole country were at the beginning considered incompetent, and, indeed, had shocking faults. However, by faithfully maintaining the principles of their art and holding them in honor, rather than indulging in their own fancies, they have become paragons of the age and teachers for all. This surely holds true for every art.

151

Someone remarked that you should give up any art of which you have not become a master by the age of fifty. At that age there is no prospect that you may acquire it by hard work. People cannot laugh at what an old man does. For him to mingle in society is unbecoming and unseemly.

It is better and more attractive as a rule if an old man stops all work and lives at leisure. A man would have to be a fool indeed to spend his whole life occupied with worldly matters. If there is something you would like to know, study it if you like, but once you have learned the general principles and your curiosity is assuaged, you should stop. Best of all is to dispense with such desires from the start.

152

The High Priest Jōnen[1] of the Saidaiji was bent of back, and his eyebrows were white; he looked truly virtuous. When he visited the palace, the Great Minister of the Center Saionji[2] exclaimed, with an air of veneration, "What an awe-inspiring figure!" Suketomo,[3] observing Saionji's deference, said, "He's old, that's all."

Some days later Suketomo appeared with a servant leading a decrepit and mangy shaggy-haired dog. "What an awe-inspiring figure he makes!" he said, offering the dog to the great minister.

1. Jōnen (1252–1331) was a priest of the Ritsu sect. Saidaiji, a temple in Nara, was a center of Ritsu discipline.
2. Saionji Sanehira (1290–1326) was the son of the man described above, sec. 114, n. 1.
3. Hino Suketomo (1290–1332) was exiled to Sado in 1324 for his complicity in a plot against the Hōjō regents, and was eventually executed there.

153

When the Major Counselor and Lay Priest Tamekane[1] had been arrested and led off to Rokuhara[2] surrounded by soldiers, Lord Suketomo saw him near Ichijō. He exclaimed, "How I envy him! What a marvelous last remembrance to have of this life!" [3]

1. Kyōgoku Tamekane (1254–1332) was twice exiled to Sado, once in 1298, and then in 1316. He was recalled by the emperor in 1303. Tamekane was the great-grandson of Fujiwara no Teika, and himself an important poet. He compiled the anthology *Gyokuyōshū* (1313–14).
2. The Hōjō regents maintained in Kyoto (at a place called Rokuhara) an office where they supervised the government of the city.
3. Suketomo thought it would be wonderful to end one's days so spectacularly; he could not foresee that he would die in a similar manner.

154

Once when Suketomo was taking shelter from the rain at the gate of the Tōji,[1] a crowd of cripples was assembled there. All were deformed: some had twisted arms or legs, others were bent backwards. Suketomo, noticing their strange appearance, thought, "Each is a unique oddity. They really are worth preserving." He gazed at them for a while, but before long the pleasure of the sight wore off, and he found them ugly and repulsive. He thought, "The best things are the most ordinary and least conspicuous." When he had returned home he realized that his recent fondness for potted plants and the pleasure he had taken especially in finding curiously twisted specimens was of the same order as his interest in the cripples. His pleasure gone, he dug up all the potted plants and threw them away.

This was quite understandable.

1. A large Shingon temple situated south of Kyoto.

155

A man who wishes to swim with the tide should first find out the prevailing moods. An untimely statement will offend the ears of the listeners and hurt their feelings, and in the end will fail to achieve its purpose. One would do well to recognize such occasions when they arise. But falling sick, bearing children, or dying—these things alone take no season into account. They never cease because the occasion is unfavorable. The truly important things—birth, growth, sickness, and death—are like the surge of a powerful river; they plunge forward on their course, never pausing an instant. That is why you may not speak of "prevailing moods" with respect to matters of real consequence, whether religious or mundane, which you are determined to carry through to completion. You may not hesitate over this or that, merely marking time.

It is not that when spring draws to a close it becomes summer, or that when summer ends the autumn comes: spring itself urges the summer to show itself; and even while the summer is still with us, the autumn is already intruding; and the chill of autumn becomes winter cold. In the tenth month there is a spell of springlike weather. The grass turns green, the plum trees bud. With the falling of the leaves, too, it is not that first the leaves fall and then young shoots form; the leaves fall because the budding from underneath is too powerful to resist. The impetus for this change being provided from underneath, the process of shifting from one to the next occurs extremely fast.

The shifts from birth to old age, from sickness to death, are even faster. The four seasons, after all, have an appointed order. The hour of death waits not its turn. Death does not necessarily come from the front; it may be stealthily planning an attack from behind. Everyone knows of death, but it comes unexpectedly, when people feel they still have time, that death is not imminent. It is like the dry flats that stretch far out into the sea, only for the tide suddenly to flood over them onto the shore.

156

It is normal that the feast a minister gives celebrating his appointment be held at an appropriate place borrowed for the occasion. The party for the minister of the left from Uji[1] was held at the East Sanjō Palace. The palace was then occupied by the emperor, but because the minister had requested it, the emperor moved elsewhere. It is the custom, though for no particular reason, to borrow the palace of the empress dowager.

1. Fujiwara no Yorinaga (1120–56), who died during the Hōgen Rebellion.

157

If we pick up a brush, we feel like writing; if we hold a musical instrument in our hands, we wish to play music. Lifting a wine cup makes us crave saké; taking up dice, we should like to play backgammon. The mind invariably reacts in this way to any stimulus. That is why we should not indulge even casually in improper amusements.

Even a perfunctory glance at one verse of some holy writing will somehow make us notice also the text that precedes and follows; it may happen then, quite suddenly, that we mend our errors of many years. Supposing we had not at that moment opened the sacred text, would we have realized our mistakes? This is a case of accidental contact producing a beneficial result. Though our hearts may not be in the least impelled by faith, if we sit before the Buddha, rosary[1] in hand, and take up a sutra, we may (even in our indolence) be accumulating merit through the act itself; though our mind may be inattentive, if we sit in meditation on a rope seat, we may enter a state of calm and concentration, without even being aware of it.

Phenomenon and essence are fundamentally one.[2] If the outward form is not at variance with the truth, an inward realization is certain to develop. We should not deny that this is true faith; we should respect and honor a conformity to truth.

1. A Buddhist rosary normally has 108 beads, one for each cause of human suffering, but some have only a fraction of that number. The rosary is rubbed in the hands as prayers are offered.
2. That is, outward actions fundamentally are the same as inward feelings. If one acts in a pious manner one's heart will be moved to piety.

158

A certain gentleman deigned to ask me, "How do you interpret the practice of emptying the saké at the bottom of the cup before offering it to someone?" I ventured to reply, "I wonder if this practice is called *gyodō*[1] because it means 'discarding what is congealed' at the bottom?" But he replied, "No, the word *gyodō* means to leave some saké to rinse the place touched by the mouth."

1. Kenkō and his interlocutors, not knowing the Chinese characters with which the sounds *gyodo* are written, guess the meaning.

159

A certain nobleman deigned to inform me, "*Minamusubi*[1] is so called because cords are repeatedly knotted together (*musubi*) to resemble the shell called *mina*." It is a mistake to say *ninamusubi*.

1. *Minamusubi* is an elaborate way of knotting a cord so that it resembles a chain or a spiral shell. The *nina* (*mina* is an archaic name) is a kind of small conch.

160

Is it wrong to call the practice of hanging a plaque over a gate "nailing"[1] it? The Kadenokōji[2] priest of the second rank used to say "hang" a plaque. Is it wrong also to speak of "nailing" the stands for viewing a festival? It is normal to say that one "nails" an awning.[3] It is better, however, to speak of "constructing" stands. To speak of "burning the sacred fire" is bad. One says "perform the rite" or "make the sacred fire." The abbot of Seikanji[4] also said, "In speaking of *gyōbō*, it is wrong to pronounce it as *gyōhō*.[5] *Gyōbō* is correct." Such instances are numerous in words we use every day.

1. I have translated *utsu* as "to nail" throughout, though this does not always make for natural expression in English. *Utsu* basically means "to hit."
2. Fujiwara no Tsunetada (1247–1320?), who became a priest in 1310. He came from a long line of calligraphers.
3. *Hirabari* was a cloth stretched flat over some poles as a sunshade.
4. Dōga Sōjō (1284–1343), who was a poet and friend of Kenkō's. Seikanji is a small Shingon temple in the hills east of Kyoto.
5. A technical term for "practice" of the Law, as opposed to teaching, etc.

161

People commonly say that the full blossoming of the cherry occurs on the 150th day after the winter solstice, or a week after the vernal equinox, but the 75th day after the beginning of spring is generally correct.

162

The sacristan of the Henjōji[1] was accustomed to feed and tame the birds on the pond. Once he spread a trail of bird feed leading into a temple building, and left one door open; then, when countless birds had flocked inside, he himself entered and, slamming shut the door, went about catching and killing the birds.

Some boys cutting grass outside heard the heartrending clamor, and told people about it. Men from the village rushed to the hall and broke inside. They saw the priest surrounded by large wild geese that were noisily flapping about, grabbing them and twisting their necks. The men seized the priest and dragged him from the temple to the police station, where he was confined to a cell, the birds he had killed hung round his neck. This happened when the Major Counselor Mototoshi was chief of police.

1. A temple west of the Hirosawa Pond in the Saga area of Kyoto.

163

The practitioners of yin-yang once had an argument as to whether or not the character *tai* in *taishō*[1] should be written with a dot. The Lay Priest Morichika said, "There is in the palace of the Konoe chancellor an astrological text in Yoshihira's[2] own hand, with a diary by an emperor on the back. In Yoshihira's text *tai* is written with a dot."

1. *Taishō* (written with a dot) was a name used by yin-yang diviners for the ninth month.
2. Abe no Yoshihira lived in the eleventh century. He was a yin-yang practitioner.

164

When people meet they are never silent a moment. There is always talk about something. If you listen to their conversations, most of what they say is meaningless chatter. Their gossip about society and their criticisms of other people cause much harm and little profit, either for themselves or others. When people are gabbling over these things, they never seem to realize that it does neither party any good.

165

It is unattractive when people mingle in a society which is not their habitual one, whether it is an easterner among people from the capital, a man from the capital who has gone to the east to make his fortune, or a priest of either an exoteric or esoteric sect[1] who has left his original faith.

1. *Kemmitsu* was a term used by Shingon priests, embracing their own esoteric (*mitsu*) doctrines and the exoteric (*ken*) doctrines of other sects.

166

When I see the things people do in their struggle to get ahead, it reminds me of someone building a snowman on a spring day, making ornaments of precious metals and stones to decorate it, and then erecting a hall. Can they wait until the hall is ready to enshrine their snowman? How often it happens that a man continues to struggle in the hope of some success, even as the life left him (which he supposes to be considerable) is melting away like a snowman, from underneath.

167

It often happens when a man involved with one art attends a performance of another art he will say, "Ah, if this were only my own art! I certainly would not sit by this way, a mere observer!" He genuinely seems to believe his words, but I find them most unattractive. If a man is jealous of the experts in an art he does not know, it would be better if he said, "I'm jealous. Why didn't I learn that?"

The man who makes a show of his own knowledge and contends with others is like a horned animal lowering its horns or a fanged animal baring its fangs. It is excellent in a man not to take pride in his good deeds and not to contend with others. An awareness of one's superiority to others is a great failing. The man who considers himself superior, whether because of his high position, his artistic skill, or the glory of his ancestors, is much to blame, even if he does not voice his pride in words but keeps it in his heart. A man must guard against feelings of superiority and forget them. Nothing makes a man appear so stupid, arouses so much criticism by others, and invites such great disasters as pride.

A man who is truly accomplished in an art is well aware of his own faults, and his aspirations being always higher than his achievements, he will never boast of himself to others.

168

When an old man has acquired surpassing ability in some art and people ask about him, "Once he has gone, who will answer our questions?" it means that he is not living in vain, for he serves as a justification for all old people. However, the very fact that his art has not deteriorated in the least makes him seem rather contemptible, for it means he has spent his whole life doing only one thing. I prefer it when an old man says, "I've forgotten it now." As a rule, even if a man knows his art, people will suspect that he is not really so talented if he keeps chattering on about it. Besides, mistakes will naturally occur. A man is more likely to seem a true master of his art if he says, "I cannot tell for certain."

It is worse still to listen to a man of eminence expatiating on some subject he knows nothing about with a look of self-satisfaction on his face; one cannot very well criticize him, but one is thinking all the while, "What nonsense!"

169

Someone said, "No one ever spoke of anything as being a 'ceremony' until the reign of Go-Saga.[1] The word has come into use in recent times." However, Kenreimon'in no Ukyō no Daibu,[2] when speaking of taking up service in the palace for a second time after the accession of Go-Toba, wrote, "How strange that the ceremonies of the court are unchanged!"

1. Reigned 1242–46. The word translated as "ceremony" is *shiki*.

2. The waiting woman of Kenreimon'in, the consort of the Emperor Takakura (reigned 1168–80). Go-Toba's reign began in 1183.

170

It is not advisable to go to someone's house without special
business. If you have gone on business, leave as soon as it is
completed. Staying for a long time can be extremely bothersome.

What a waste of time it is for both parties when people
sit down for a chat! Words multiply; the body becomes
fatigued; the mind is agitated; and time is spent to the
detriment of everything else. But it is bad also to begrudge
words. If a subject should come up which you dislike, it is
best to say so plainly.

We must make an exception about staying long in a case
when you are conversing with someone after your heart and,
having nothing else to do, he says, "Please stay a while
longer—today, let's have a quiet talk." Everyone must at
times show Juan Chi's[1] brown eyes of welcome.

It is most agreeable when a visitor comes without business, talks pleasantly for a while, then leaves. I am extremely
pleased too when I receive a letter saying merely, "I'm writing because it's been such a long time."

1. Juan Chi was one of the Seven Sages of the Bamboo Forest. He was
said to have shown "brown eyes" to people he liked and "white eyes" to
those he disliked.

It happened once that a man playing at matching shells[1] took no notice of the shells before him, but was so busy looking to the side and darting glances behind people's sleeves and even into their laps that in the meantime the shells before him were covered by another player. The good players do not seem to strain themselves to capture shells from a distance, but though they appear to match only those nearby, they cover a great many.

If, when you have placed your counter in your corner of the board, you keep your eyes on your opponent's pieces as you flip your counter,[2] you will never score a hit. You should look carefully at your own piece and aim it straight along the line of the board closest to you; you will then be sure to hit the other piece.

We should not look to distant places for advantage; whatever the case may be, make sure that matters closest to hand are properly dealt with. There is a saying of the Duke Ch'ing Hsien,[3] "Do what is good and ask not about what follows." Doubtless this holds true too of governing a country. When a ruler pays no heed to nearby matters and incites disorder by his careless and willful acts, even distant provinces will surely rebel. Only then will he seek counter-measures, in the manner of the dictum found in a medical book:[4] "The foolish man sleeps in a place exposed to the wind and damp, then asks divine help to cure his sickness." Such a ruler does not realize how far afield his influence will spread if he brings surcease to the grief of the people within his ken, practices charity, and acts with justice. Yü went to conquer the three Miao tribes,[5] but this was not as effective as when he withdrew his army and promulgated good works.

1. *Kai-ōi* was a game in which players tried to "match" or "cover" shells in the possession of an opponent.
2. The precise nature of this game is unknown, but we can guess from the description how it was played.
3. Also known as Chao Pien (1008–84), an official who served under three emperors of the Sung dynasty. He was known for his noble character.
4. Commentators have identified this book as *Pên-ts'ao-ching*, a pharmaceutical botany text attributed to the legendary Emperor Shen Nung, but apparently a forgery of the Later Han dynasty.
5. The deeds of the legendary Emperor Yü are described in *Shu Ching*.

172

When a man is young he has such an overabundance of energy that his senses are quickly stirred and he has many desires. It is as easy for him to put himself in danger and court destruction as to roll a ball. He likes beautiful clothes and possessions, and spends his fortune on them, only to abandon everything for the shabby black robes of a priest. Or, his abundance of high spirits may lead him to quarrel, only to feel ashamed in his heart and envious of his antagonist; his uncertain whims shift from day to day. Now giving himself to his lusts, now moved by others' kindness, now performing some generous action, he yearns, when he hears stories of men who ruined or even destroyed lives that might have lasted a hundred years, to do the same, and never gives a thought to leading a safe and long life. He is drawn wherever his fancies lead him, and becomes the subject of gossip that lasts even after his death. Youth is the time when a man ruins himself.

An old man's spirit grows feeble; he is indifferent and slow to respond, unmoved by everything. His mind being naturally placid, he engages in no useless activities. He takes good care of himself, is untroubled by worries, and is careful not to be a nuisance to others. The old are as superior to the young in wisdom as the young are superior to the old in looks.

173

Information about Ono no Komachi[1] is exceedingly unreliable. A description of her appearance in old age is found in the essay called *Tamatsukuri.*[2] This essay, according to one theory, was written by Kiyoyuki,[3] but it is included in a catalogue of works by Kōbō Daishi. Kōbō died at the beginning of the Jōwa era.[4] Was not the prime of Komachi's life after that date? Obviously, something is wrong.

1. A poet of the early Heian period. Legends about her life gave rise to various Nō plays.
2. A reference to *Tamatsukuri Komachi Sōsuisho,* an essay and poem written in Chinese, probably in the eleventh century. The traditional attributions to Kōbō Daishi or Miyoshi Kiyoyuki are obviously wrong. A more recent theory attributes the work to Fujiwara no Akihira (989–1066).
3. Miyoshi Kiyoyuki (847–918), a scholar and statesman.
4. The Jōwa era was 834–48. Kōbō lived from 774 to 835.

174

If, when hunting with falcons, you use a dog that has been trained to hunt with small hawks, he becomes useless for hawking. It is certainly true that once one occupies oneself with the big, one loses interest in the small. Among all the many activities of man, none gives profounder pleasure than delight in the Way. This truly is the matter of greatest importance. If a man once hears about the Way and sets his heart on it, what enterprise will he not forsake? To what other activity will he devote his energies? Is a man, however foolish, likely to be inferior in intellect to the cleverest dog?

175

There are many things in the world I cannot understand. I cannot imagine why people find it so enjoyable to press liquor on you the first thing, on every occasion, and force you to drink it. The drinker's face grimaces as if with unbearable distress, and he looks for a chance to get rid of the drink and escape unobserved, only to be stopped and senselessly forced to drink more. As a result, even dignified men suddenly turn into lunatics and behave idiotically, and men in the prime of health act like patients afflicted with grave illnesses and collapse unconscious before one's eyes. What a scandalous way to spend a day of celebration! The victim's head aches even the following day, and he lies abed, groaning, unable to eat, unable to recall what happened the day before, as if everything had taken place in a previous incarnation. He neglects important duties, both public and private, and the result is disaster. It is cruel and a breach of courtesy to oblige a man to undergo such experiences. Moreover, will not the man who has been put through this ordeal feel bitter and resentful towards his tormentors? If it were reported that such a custom, unknown among ourselves, existed in some foreign country, we should certainly find it peculiar and even incredible.

I find this practice distressing to observe even in strangers. A man whose thoughtful manner had seemed attractive laughs and shouts uncontrollably; he chatters interminably, his court cap askew, the cords of his cloak undone, the skirts of his kimono rolled up to his shins, presenting so disreputable a picture that he is unrecognizable as his usual self. A woman will brush the hair away from her forehead and brazenly lift up her face with a roar of laughter. She clings to a man's hand as he holds a saké cup, and if badly bred she will push appetizers into the mouth of her companion, or her own, a disgraceful sight. Some men shout at the top of their lungs, singing and dancing, each to his own tune. Sometimes an old priest, invited at the behest of a distinguished guest, strips to the waist, revealing grimy, sallow skin, and twists his body in a manner so revolting that even those watching with amusement are nauseated. Some drone on about their achievements, boring their listeners; others weep drunkenly. People of the lower classes swear at one another and quarrel in a shocking and frightening manner; after various shameful and wretched antics they end up by grabbing things they have been refused, or falling from the verandah (or from a horse or a carriage) and injuring themselves. Or, if they are not sufficiently important to ride, they stagger along the main thoroughfares and perform various unmentionable acts before earthen walls or at people's gates. It is most upsetting to see an old priest in his shawl leaning on the shoulder of a boy and staggering along, mumbling something incomprehensible.

If such behavior were of benefit either in this world or the next, there might be some excuse. It is, however, the source of numerous calamities in this world, destroying fortunes and inviting sickness. They call liquor the chief of all medicines, but it is, in fact, the origin of all sicknesses. Liquor makes you forget your unhappiness, we are told, but when a man is drunk he may remember even his past griefs and weep over them. As for the future life, liquor deprives a man of his wisdom and consumes his good actions like fire; he therefore increases the burden of sin, violates many commandments and, in the end, drops into hell. Buddha taught that a man who takes liquor and forces another to drink will be reborn five hundred times without hands.[1]

Though liquor is as loathsome as I have described it, there naturally are some occasions when it is hard to dispense with. On a moonlit night, a morning after a snowfall, or under the cherry blossoms, it adds to our pleasure if, while chatting at our ease, we bring forth the wine cups. Liquor is cheering on days when we are bored, or when a friend pays an unexpected visit. It is exceedingly agreeable too when you are offered cakes and wine most elegantly from behind a screen of state by a person of quality you do not know especially well. In winter it is delightful to sit opposite an intimate friend in a small room, toasting something to eat over the fire, and to drink deeply together. It is pleasant also when stopping briefly on a journey, or picnicking in the countryside, to sit drinking on the grass, saying all the while, "I wish we had something to eat with this saké." It is amusing when a man who hates liquor has been made to drink a little. How pleasing it is, again, when some distinguished man deigns to say, "Have another. Your cup looks a little empty." I am happy when some man I have wanted to make my friend is fond of liquor, and we are soon on intimate terms.

Despite all I have said, a drinker is amusing, and his offense is pardonable. It happens sometimes that a guest who has slept late in the morning is awakened by his host flinging open the sliding doors. The startled guest, his face still dazed by sleep, pokes out his head with its thin topknot and, not stopping to put on his clothes, carries them off in his arms, trailing some behind as he flees. It is an amusing and appropriate finale to the drinking party to catch a glimpse of the skinny, hairy shanks he reveals from behind as he lifts his skirts in flight.

1. So stated in the Bommō-kyō (Brahmajāla sūtra), a sutra translated into Chinese by Kumārajīva in 406.

176

The Black Chamber[1] is a room where the emperor from Komatsu[2] after his accession to the throne always cooked for himself, still remembering how in the past, when he was a private person, he had dabbled in cookery. They say it is called the Black Chamber because it has become sooty from kindling smoke.

1. The Black Chamber (kurodo) was a room in the Seiryōden (sovereign's residential palace).
2. The Emperor Kōkō (830–87) succeeded to the throne in 884.

177

Once when there was a football match at the house of Prince Munetaka,[1] the minister of central affairs, in Kamakura, the grounds were still wet after a rain. There was a discussion as to what should be done. Sasaki, the lay priest from Oki,[2] presented the prince with a cartful of sawdust, which was spread over the entire field. There were no further difficulties on account of the mud. "It's amazing he should have been prepared for such an emergency," people exclaimed in admiration.

When a certain person later referred to the incident, the middle counselor from Yoshida[3] said, "It surprises me he hadn't any dry sand ready." I felt ashamed of my earlier admiration. The sawdust which had so impressed me was a crude and irregular expedient. I recalled that it was the old custom for groundkeepers charged with football fields to be provided with dry sand.

1. Prince Munetaka (1243–74) was the eldest son of the Emperor Go-Saga.
2. Sasaki Masayoshi (1208–90).
3. Probably Fujiwara no Fuyukata, who took Buddhist orders in 1329 at the age of forty-four.

178

The retainers of a certain noble family, having witnessed a performance of *kagura* in the palace, were describing it to someone. "Such and such a gentleman carried the Sacred Sword,"[1] they said. A palace lady in waiting, hearing this remark, whispered, "When His Majesty visits another part of the palace, the sword from his daytime pavilion is carried." I was charmed by her discretion. I gather she had long been in service in the palace.

1. One of the three imperial regalia.

179

The High Priest Dōgen,[1] a monk who had studied in China, brought back with him a set of the Tripitaka which he kept at a place called Yakeno near Rokuhara. He was especially given to lecturing on the Surangama Sutra, and called his temple the Naranda.[2] The holy man said, "There is a tradition that Ōe no Masafusa[3] believed the Great Gate of the Nālanda Monastery in India faced north, but I can find absolutely nothing in the *Record of the Western Borders* or the *Travels* by Fa-hsien[4] to confirm this. I wonder on what authority Masafusa made this statement. It is highly dubious. The Hsi-ming Temple[5] in China of course faces north."

1. A Zen priest, not to be confused with the Dōgen who founded the Sōtō branch of the Zen sect.
2. Named after the Nālanda Monastery at Bihar in India, a great center of Buddhist studies to which students from distant countries flocked.
3. An important scholar of the Heian period, who was born in 1041 and died in 1111.
4. *Hsi Yü Chi* (Record of the western borders) by Hsüan-tsang and *Fa-hsien Chuan* (Travels of *Fa-hsien*) are both records of journeys to India by Chinese pilgrims.
5. A temple built in 658 by order of the Emperor Kao Tsung in Ch'ang-an, along the lines of the Jetavana vihara in India.

180

By *sagichō* is meant taking the mallets used at the New Year games from the Shingon-in to the Shinsen garden[1] and burning them there. The refrain people sing at the time, "In the pond that prayer provided," refers to the pond in the Shinsen garden.

1. The Shingon-in was a place of worship inside the palace. The Shinsen-en, the emperor's garden, still survives in a sadly reduced state.

181

The meaning of the word *koyuki* in the song, *"Fure, fure, koyuki, Tamba no koyuki,"* is "powder-snow," used because the snow falls like rice powder after pounding and husking. The second line, which should be *tamare koyuki* has been corrupted to *Tamba no koyuki.*[1] One authority has claimed that the line after that should be, "On fences and the crotches of trees." I wonder if this expression dates back to antiquity. The Emperor Toba, as a boy, used *koyuki* to describe falling snow, as we know from the diary of Sanuki no Suke.[2]

1. *Tamare koyuki* seems to be a command, "Pile up, powder-snow!" *Tamba no koyuki* is "powder-snow from Tamba." Tamba was the province lying west of Kyoto. It may have been thought that snow originated in that direction.
2. Sanuki no Suke was a court lady, the daughter of Fujiwara no Akitsuna (1029–1103). Her diary was apparently written between 1107 and 1110. The passage referred to is from 1108.

182

Lord Takachika,[1] the Shijō major counselor, offered some dried salmon for the imperial table. Someone objected, "Who ever heard of His Majesty eating such a common dish?" The major counselor replied, "You might say that if His Majesty never ate salmon in any form, but since this is not the case, what objection can there be to dried salmon?

Surely you don't pretend that His Majesty never eats dried trout."

1. Fujiwara no Takachika (1203–79).

183

People cut off the horns of a bull that charges and clip the ears of a horse that bites, as a warning sign. The owner is committing a crime if he fails to give this warning and allows his bull or horse to harm people. One should not keep a dog that bites people. These are all offenses prohibited by law.

184

The mother of Tokiyori,[1] the governor of Sagami, was called the Zen nun of Matsushita. Once, when she had invited the governor to her hermitage, the nun herself took a small knife and cut around the broken places in the paper *shōji,* repairing them with new paper. Her brother Yoshikage, the vice-governor of Akita Castle,[2] who was there preparing the reception for that day, said, "Let me do it. I'll have a servant of mine repair the *shōji.* He knows all about such things." She replied, "I'm sure your servant's work wouldn't be any better than mine." She went on papering the *shōji,* one pane at a time. Yoshikage, pursuing the matter, said, "It would be far easier to repaper the whole *shōji* at one time. Besides, don't you think it looks patchy and ugly this way?" "I intend to repaper the whole thing after his visit, but I've purposely chosen to do it this way, just for today. I would like to have the young man notice this and realize that it is possible to go on using things by repairing just the broken parts." This was a most impressive gesture.

The art of governing a country is founded on thrift. The nun, though a woman, acted in keeping with the spirit of the sages. Truly, she was no ordinary woman, for she had as her son a man who preserved the order of the state.

1. Hōjō Tokiyori (1227–63) was the fifth regent (*shikken*) for the Kamakura shogunate.
2. Adachi Yoshikage was appointed vice-governor of Akita Castle in 1218.

185

Yasumori, the vice-governor of Akita Castle[1] and governor of Mutsu, was an incomparable horseman. Once, when he had ordered that a certain horse be brought out for him, he noticed how the horse jumped over the doorsill, its legs together. He said, "This horse is high-strung," and had his saddle placed on another horse. The other horse was brought out. This one kept its legs extended when it came to the doorsill and kicked against it. Yasumori said, "This horse is slow-witted. He'll surely be in an accident." He refused to mount either horse.

Who but an expert in the art would have been so afraid?

1. Adachi Yasumori (1231–85) was the son of Yoshikage. He became vice-governor of Akita Castle in 1254 and rose in 1282 to be governor of Mutsu. He and his family were executed in 1285.

186

Yoshida, the horseman, once said, "Every horse has its quirks. One should recognize that a man is no match in strength for an obstinate horse. Before getting on a horse, you should examine it carefully and find out its strong and weak points. Next, see whether or not there is anything dangerous about the bit or saddle gear. If anything disturbs you, you should not ride the horse. The man who does not forget these cautions deserves to be called a horseman. This is the secret of riding."

187

In any art the specialist, even if he is unskillful, is always superior to the most talented amateur. This is the difference between the man who is habitually cautious and never rash, and the man who does whatever suits his pleasure.

This is true not only of the arts and crafts; the source of success in the actions and calculations of daily life is to be dull and cautious. To be clever and willful is the source of failure.

188

A certain man, deciding to make his son a priest, said, "You will study and learn the principle of Cause and Effect, and you will then preach sermons to earn a livelihood." The son, doing as instructed, learned how to ride a horse as a first step towards becoming a preacher. He thought that when

people wanted him to conduct a service they would probably send a horse for him, since he owned neither a palan-
quin nor a carriage, and it would be embarrassing if, because
of his awkwardness in the saddle, he fell from the horse.
Next, thinking that if, after the service, he were offered
some saké and had no social graces to display, the donor
would be disappointed, he learned to sing popular songs.
When he was at last able to pass muster in these two arts, he
felt anxious to attain real proficiency. He devoted himself so
diligently to his practice that he had no time to learn preach-
ing, and in the meantime he had grown old.

This priest was not the only one; the story is typical of
people in general. When they are young they are concerned
about the projects they foresee lying ahead of them in the
distant future—establishing themselves in different professions and carrying out some great undertaking, mastering
an art, acquiring learning—but they think of their lives as
stretching out indefinitely, and idly allow themselves to be
constantly distracted by things directly before their eyes. They
pass months and days in this manner, succeeding in none of
their plans, and so they grow old. In the end, they neither
become proficient in their profession, nor do they gain the
eminence they anticipated. However they regret it, they
cannot roll back the years, but decline more and more
rapidly, like a wheel rolling downhill.

In view of the above, we must carefully compare in our
minds all the different things in life we might hope to make
our principal work, and decide which is of the greatest
value; this decided, we should renounce our other interests
and devote ourselves to that one thing only. Many projects
present themselves in the course of a day or even an hour;
we must perform those that offer even slightly greater ad-

vantages, renouncing the others and giving ourselves entirely to whatever is most important. If we remain attached to them all, and are reluctant to give up any, we will not accomplish a single thing.

It is like a *go* player who, not wasting a move, gets the jump on his opponent by sacrificing a small advantage to achieve a great one. It is easy, of course, to sacrifice three stones in order to gain ten. The hard thing is to sacrifice ten stones in order to gain eleven. A man should be ready to choose the course which is superior even by one stone, but when it comes to sacrificing ten, he feels reluctant, and it is hard to make an exchange which will not yield many additional stones. If we hesitate to give up what we have, and at the same time are eager to grab what the other man holds, we shall certainly fail to get his pieces and lose our own.

A man living in the capital has urgent business in the Eastern Hills, and has already reached the house of his destination when it occurs to him that if he goes to the Western Hills he may reap greater advantage; in that case, he should turn back at the gate and proceed to the Western Hills. If, however, he thinks, "I've come all this way. I might as well take care of my business here first. There was no special day set for my business in the Western Hills. I'll go there some other time, after I have returned," the sloth of a moment will turn in this manner into the sloth of an entire lifetime. This is to be dreaded.

If you are determined to carry out one particular thing, you must not be upset that other things fall through. Nor should you be embarrassed by other people's laughter. A great enterprise is unlikely to be achieved except at the sacrifice of everything else.

Once, at a large gathering, a certain man said, "Some people say *masuho no susuki*, others say *masoho no susuki*.[1] The holy man of Watanabe knows the secret tradition of this pronunciation." The priest Tōren,[2] who was present at the gathering and heard this remark, said (it being raining at the time), "Has anyone a raincoat and umbrella he can lend me? I intend to call on this holy man of Watanabe and find out about the *susuki*." People said, "You shouldn't get so excited. Wait till the rain stops." The priest replied, "What a foolish thing to say! Do you suppose that a man's life will wait for the rain to clear? If I should die or the priest passes away in the meantime, could I inquire about it then?" So saying, he hurried out and went to study the tradition. This struck me as a most unusual and valid story.

It is written in the *Analects*[3] that "in speed there is success." Just as Tōren was impatient to learn about the *susuki*, we should be impatient to discover the sources of enlightenment.

1. *Susuki* is a variety of pampas grass. *Masuho no susuki* has been identified as *susuki* with a plume about a foot long; *masoho no susuki* as *susuki* with tangled plumes; and *masuu no susuki* as *susuki* of russet tinge. The ability to make such distinctions was accounted a mastery of the secrets of the art of poetry; hence, Tōren's alacrity.
2. A poet of some distinction, but no biographical data is known.
3. *Analects* XVII, 6: "He who is diligent succeeds in all he undertakes" (Waley). Here again, Kenkō's interpretation of the Chinese text is at variance with the present one.

189

You may intend to do something today, only for pressing business to come up unexpectedly and take up all of your attention the rest of the day. Or a person you have been expecting is prevented from coming, or someone you hadn't expected comes calling. The thing you have counted on goes amiss, and the thing you had no hopes for is the only one to succeed. A matter which promised to be a nuisance passes off smoothly, and a matter which should have been easy proves a great hardship. Our daily experiences bear no resemblance to what we had anticipated. This is true throughout the year, and equally true for our entire lives. But if we decide that everything is bound to go contrary to our anticipations, we discover that naturally there are also some things which do not contradict expectations. This makes it all the harder to be definite about anything. The one thing you can be certain of is the truth that all is uncertainty.

190

A man should never marry. I am charmed when I hear a man say, "I am still living alone." When I hear someone say, "He has married into so and so's family" or "He has taken such and such a wife and they are living together," I feel nothing but contempt for the man. He will be ridiculed by others too, who will say, "No doubt he thought that commonplace woman was quite a catch, and that's why he took her off with him." Or, if the woman happens to be beautiful, they are sure to feel, "He dotes on her so much that he worships her as his private Buddha. Yes, that's no doubt the case."

The woman who cleverly manages a household is the least agreeable to her husband. It is exasperating to see the pains and affection she lavishes on her children when they are born; and after her husband has died she will become a nun and look so decrepit that it will be positively shocking.

Living day in and day out with a woman, no matter what she may be like, is bound to be frustrating and the source of irritation. The woman too is likely to feel insecure. The relationship, however, can last unbroken for many years if the couple lives apart, and the man only occasionally visits or stays with the woman. If the man casually visits the woman and remains with her just temporarily, a freshness will cling to their romance.

191

I feel sorry for the man who says that night dims the beauty of things. At night colors, ornaments, and richness of materials show to their best advantage. By day you should wear simple, conservative clothes, but at night showy, flashy costumes are most attractive. This holds true of people's appearance too: lamplight makes a beautiful face seem even more beautiful, and a voice heard in the dark—a voice that betrays a fear of being overheard—is endearing. Perfumes and the sound of music too are best at night.

It is charming if, on a night which is not any special occasion, a visitor arriving at the palace after it has grown quite late appears in splendid attire. Young people, being observant of one another irrespective of the time of day, should always be dressed in their best, with no distinction of formal and informal attire, above all when they are most at their ease. How pleasant it is when a handsome man grooms his hair after dark, or a woman, late at night, slips from an audience chamber and, mirror in hand, touches up her make-up before she appears again.

192

Visits to shrines and temples are best made on days when others do not go, and by night.

193

When an ignorant man sizes up somebody and thinks he has discovered how much the other man knows, he is unlikely ever to be correct. It is a grave misconception for a stupid man who has one skill, playing *go,* when he meets an intelligent man with no talent for this game, to decide that the man is no match for himself in learning; or for an expert in one of the many different arts, seeing that others are ignorant of his particular specialty, to conclude that he is more accomplished than they. If one priest devotes himself exclusively to scriptural study and another practices Zen meditation, each, judging the other, would conclude that he was inferior, and both would be wrong. One must not dispute the merits or criticize anything outside one's own field.

194

The powers of observation of an intelligent man are unlikely to be at all mistaken.

If, for example, a certain man invents falsehoods and spreads them with the intent of deceit, some people will innocently suppose that he speaks the truth and be hoodwinked by his words; others will be so deeply convinced that they will think up an annoying variety of lies to add to the original one. Still others, unimpressed by the lie, will pay it no attention. Yet others will be rather suspicious and ponder over the story, neither believing nor disbelieving. Others, though they find the lie improbable, will nevertheless decide it may be true, if only because people are spreading it, and let the matter go at that. There will be people too who make all sorts of guesses and pretend they have caught onto the truth, nodding and smiling knowingly, but who in fact understand nothing. Others will deduce the truth, and think, "I'm sure that's what happened," but hesitate, for fear they may be mistaken. Some will clap their hands and laugh, saying there is nothing new in this lie.

Some too, though aware of the truth, will not reveal they have caught on, nor make comments one way or the other on what they realize is the truth, acting as if they were ignorant of the facts. Finally, there are those who, knowing from the start the purpose of the lie, do not ridicule it in any way, but on the contrary sympathize with the man who invented it, and join forces with him.

The man who can detect truth from falsehood even in the pleasantries of fools should have no difficulty in ascertaining from their words and their facial expressions their different reactions to a lie. How much easier is it, then, for the truly enlightened man to see through us deluded creatures; it is like looking at something in the palm of his hand. But we should refrain from using the same principles of deduction to make pronouncements on the Buddhist parables.[1]

1. In other words, some parables and other Buddhist writings are difficult to accept as truth, but they should not be dismissed as lies.

195

A certain man was traveling along the Koga High Road [1] when he saw a person wearing a *kosode* and *ōguchi*[2] dipping a wooden carving of Jizō in the water of a rice paddy and carefully washing it. As he watched, baffled, two or three men in *kariginu*[3] appeared and said, "Here he is!" They took the man off with them. He was the great minister of the center from Koga,[4] a truly impressive man when in his right mind.

1. A straight road going from Ōyamazaki to Koga, west of Kyoto.
2. A *kosode* is a kimono with short sleeves, and an *ōguchi* the divided skirt of stiff silk commonly worn in Nō plays. Both articles of dress mark the wearer as a person of quality who should not have been in a rice paddy.
3. Ordinary attire of members of the upper classes. The men are presumably retainers who have come in search of their aberrant master.
4. Minamoto no Michimoto (1240–1308), who became great minister of the center (*naidaijin*) in 1288.

196

When the sacred car of the Tōdaiji was returned to its seat from the Wakamiya Shrine at the Eastern Temple, the nobles of the Minamoto clan accompanied it. The Koga great minister, then a general, led the van, clearing the way. The prime minister from Tsuchimikado[1] asked, "Do you think it is suitable to clear the way before a shrine?" The great minister replied merely, "It is my business as a military official to know how guards are supposed to behave."

Later Koga remarked, "The prime minister has read *Ho-kuzanshō* but is unacquainted with the opinions in the *Sei-*

kyū.[2] It is particularly fitting for us to clear the way before a shrine because we fear evil demons and spirits of the same family as the enshrined god."

1. Minamoto no Sadazane (1241–1306) became prime minister in 1301.
2. *Hokuzanshō*, a book of court ceremonial and precedent, was compiled by Fujiwara no Kintō (966–1041). It discusses the question of whether or not the sacred car should be escorted by guards when passing a shrine. *Seikyū* (or possibly *Saikyū*) refers to *Seikyūki*, the standard work on court ceremonials of the early Heian period, by Minamoto no Takaakira (914–982). *Seikyūki*, however, offers no justification for an armed guard escorting the car.

197

The words "fixed complement"[1] are used not only about priests at the various temples but in the *Engishiki*[2] for female officials of lower rank. The words must have been a common designation for all officials whose numbers were fixed.

1. *Jōgaku.*
2. A work in fifty chapters on ceremonials, administration, court usage, etc., completed in 927.

198

There are honorary officials not only of the second rank but also of the fourth rank. It is so recorded in *Essentials of Statesmanship.*[1]

1. *Seiji Yōryaku*, a work on legal institutions, compiled about 1010 by Koremune Masasuke.

199

The Abbot Gyōsen of Yokawa[1] said, "China is the land of *ryo* mode. They do not employ the *ritsu*[2] mode. In Japan we have only the *ritsu* and not the *ryo*."

1. Gyōsen Hōin apparently flourished in the late thirteenth century. Yokawa is one of three pagodas on Mount Hiei.
2. Both modes were in fact used in Japan, but *ritsu* exclusively for the *shōmyō* (Buddhist chants).

200

Kure bamboo has narrow leaves, river bamboo has broad leaves. In the palace you will find river bamboo near the moat; *kure* bamboo has been planted by the Jijū Hall.

201

There were two stupas: the one at the bottom of the mountain was called Gejō, the one near the top, Taibon.[1]

1. Gejō and Taibon were stupas on Ryōshusen (Gṛdhrakūṭa in Sanskrit), a mountain whose name means Eagle Peak. Buddha taught on this mountain. *Gejō* means "to descend from a chariot," and the stupa marked the place where the king proceeded on foot; *taibon* means "to withdraw from the common herd."

202

There is no documentary evidence to support the popular belief that, the tenth month being the "godless" month, we should abstain from religious ceremonies at that time. Nor are references ever cited. I wonder if the name came into being because no festivals were held at the various shrines during that month?

Some hold that in the "godless" month the gods all gather at the Great Shrine of Ise,[1] but I can find no authority for this. If this were true, the month should be one of special festivities at Ise, but again, there is no record to that effect. There are many instances of imperial visits to shrines during the "godless" month, but most were inauspicious.

1. Normally it was believed that the gods gathered that month at Izumo, not at Ise.

203

Nobody is left who knows the proper manner of hanging a quiver before the house of a man in disgrace with His Majesty. Formerly, it was the custom to hang a quiver at the Tenjin Shrine on Gojō when the emperor was ill or when a general epidemic was rampant. The deity of the Yugi Shrine[1] at Kurama is another god before whom quivers were hung. If a quiver carried by a police officer was hung before a man's house, no one could enter or leave. Ever since this practice died out it has been customary to place a seal on a house.

1. The name Yugi is the homophone of *yugi,* or "quiver." The Yugi Shrine is situated within the Kurama Temple.

204

A criminal being flogged with rods is placed on a torture rack and tied to it. Today no one knows the shape of the rack nor the manner of attaching the criminal.

205

The practice on Mount Hiei of making written oaths in the name of the Great Teacher[1] began with the Abbot Jie.[2] Written oaths are of no concern to the legal experts. During the holy reigns of the past no governmental functions were carried out with reference to written oaths, but in recent times the practice has become prevalent.

Again, the laws do not recognize pollution of water or fire. The pollution must be in the containing vessels.

1. Great Teacher (*daishi*) designates Dengyō Daishi (Saichō), the founder of the monastery on Mount Hiei.
2. Jie Sōjō (912–85), the eighteenth chief abbot (*zasu*) of Mount Hiei.

206

Once, when the Tokudaiji minister of the right[1] was chief of the imperial police, he was holding a meeting of his staff at the middle gate when an ox belonging to an official named Akikane got loose and wandered into the ministry building. It climbed up on the dais where the chief was seated and lay there, chewing its cud. Everyone was sure that this was some grave portent, and urged that the ox be sent to a yin-yang diviner. However, the prime minister, the father of the minister of the right,[2] said, "An ox has no discrimination. It has legs—there is nowhere it won't go. It does not make sense to deprive an underpaid official of the wretched ox he needs in order to attend court." He returned the ox to its owner and changed the matting on which it had lain. No untoward event of any kind occurred afterwards.

They say that if you see a prodigy and do not treat it as such, its character as a prodigy is destroyed.

1. Fujiwara no Kintaka. See sec. 23, n. 31.
2. Fujiwara no Sanetomo (1202–65).

207

When they were leveling the ground to build the Kameyama palace, they came on a mound where a huge number of large snakes were coiled together. They decided that these snakes were the gods of the place and reported this to His Majesty. He asked, "What should be done about it?" People all said, "These snakes have occupied the place since ancient times. It would be wrong to root them up recklessly." But the prime minister said, "What curse would creatures dwelling on imperial property place on the site of a new palace? Supernatural beings are without malice; they surely will not wreak any punishment. We should get rid of all the snakes." The workmen destroyed the mound and released the snakes into the Ōi River. No curse whatsoever resulted.

208

When tying the string round a sutra scroll, it is usual to cross the string from top to bottom, to form a kind of *tasuki*,[1] to loop the end, then pass the end of the loop sideways under the crossed parts. The Abbot Kōshun of the Kegon-in² once unfastened a string tied in this manner, and tied it over again. He explained, "This style is a recent corruption and most unattractive. The proper way is simply to pass the string round and round the scroll from top to bottom, and to insert the loop at the end through the string." He was an old man and well-versed in such matters.

1. A *tasuki* is a cord which is crossed and looped around both sleeves of a kimono so that the sleeves will not get in the way. The crossing of the string presumably suggests a *tasuki*.
2. The Kegon-in was a part of Ninnaji. All we know about Kōshun Sōjō is that he presided over ceremonies held in 1320 and 1323.

209

A man went to court over ownership of another man's rice field. He lost his suit and was so disappointed that he sent some laborers to harvest the crop in the field and bring it to him. The men first of all went about harvesting some other fields on the way. Somebody objected, "This isn't the disputed field. What are you doing here?" The reapers answered, "There is no reason to harvest the crop on that field either. As long as we have come to do a senseless thing, what difference does it make which field we reap?" Their logic was most peculiar.

210

All we know about the *yobukodori*¹ is that it is a bird associated with spring, but nothing in writing plainly indicates to what species it belongs. In a certain Shingon text there is a section describing the rites for summoning the soul that are observed when a *yobukodori* has sung. This refers to a *nue*,[2] a night bird. In a *chōka* of the *Manyōshū*[3] the *nue* is mentioned after a verse saying, "A long spring day when the mists rise." This would suggest that the *nue* resembled the *yobukodori* in its season too.

1. People now conjecture that the *yobukodori* was a kind of nightingale, but its identity has been debated for 500 years. It was one of three birds mentioned in *Kokinshū* about which secret traditions were compiled.
2. The *nue*, a kind of blackbird, was considered a bird of ill-omen.
3. Reference is made to the poem by Prince Ikusa beginning, "Not knowing that the long spring day—the misty day—is spent,/Like the 'night thrush' I grieve within me . . ." *Nue* is here translated "night thrush."

211

We cannot trust in anything. The foolish man places great trust in things, and this sometimes leads to bitterness and anger.

If you have power, do not trust in it; powerful men are the first to fall. You may have many possessions, but they are not to be depended on; they are easily lost in a moment. Nor should you trust in your learning if you have any; even Confucius was not favored by his times. You may have virtue, but you must not rely on it; even Yen Hui was unlucky.[1] Do not trust in the favor of your lord; his punishment may strike before you know it. You cannot depend on your servants either; they will disobey you and run away. Nor should you trust in another person's kind feelings; they will certainly change. Do not rely on promises; it is rare for people to be sincere.

If you trust neither in yourself nor in others, you will rejoice when things go well, but bear no resentment when they go badly. You will then have room on either side to expand, and not be constrained. With nothing too close before or behind you, you will not be blocked. When a man is cramped for space, he is broken and crushed. When the activity of the mind is constricted and rigid, a man will come into collision with things at every turn and be harmed by disputes. If you have space for maneuvering and are flexible, not one hair will be harmed.

Man is the most miraculous of creatures within heaven and earth. Heaven and earth are boundless. Why should man's nature be dissimilar? When it is generous and unconstrained, joy and anger cannot hamper it, and it remains unaffected by externals.

1. A virtuous pupil of Confucius, who died young.

212

The autumn moon is incomparably beautiful. Any man who supposes the moon is always the same, regardless of the season, and is therefore unable to detect the difference in autumn, must be exceedingly insensitive.

213

Fire tongs are never used when placing lighted charcoal in a *hibachi* in the presence of the emperor or empress. It must be transferred directly from an earthenware vessel. The charcoal must therefore be properly stacked, taking care that none drop from the vessel.

On the occasion of an imperial visit to Yawata an attendant, dressed in spotless white, used his hands to put charcoal on the fire. A certain expert in court ceremonial remarked, "There is no objection to using fire tongs when one is wearing white."

214

The music called *Sōfuren* (Love for a husband) is not so named because of a woman's love for a man. Originally the title was written with characters meaning "The Lotus by the Premier's Office." The similarity in sound gave rise to the confusion. The music dates from the days when Wang Chien of Chin[1] became a counselor and planted lotuses for his delectation. From that time on the office of the minister was known as the "Lotus Hall." The music known as *Kaikotsu* (Turn abruptly) should be *Kaikotsu,* the name of the land of the Uigurs, a powerful barbarian state. These barbarians came to China after their surrender to the Han people, and played the music of their country.

1. Wang Chien (452–510) in 485 converted his house into a public office.

215

Taira no Nobutoki Ason[1] in his old age used to tell this story about former days. "I was summoned one evening by the Saimyōji lay priest.[2] I said I would go to him immediately, but having no fresh ceremonial costume to wear, I was dawdling over one thing and another when he sent a second message asking, 'Is it that you have no *hitatare*[3] to wear? It

doesn't matter how peculiar a costume you wear at this hour
—it's night, after all. Hurry.' I accordingly went to court in
the rumpled *hitatare* I usually wore at home. When I arrived
the lay priest brought out a wine jar and some earthenware
cups, explaining, 'It would have been lonely drinking this
saké by myself, so I sent for you. I'm afraid, though, I haven't
a thing to eat with it. Everybody must be in bed by now.
Would you look around and see if you can find something
suitable to eat?' I lit a taper and searched in every corner until I finally discovered on a shelf in the kitchen an unglazed
jar with a little bean paste sticking to the bottom. I offered
this to His Excellency, saying, 'This is all I could find.' 'That
will do quite nicely,' he said, and good-naturedly drank a
number of cups of wine, which made him quite mellow.
That's how things were in the old days," Nobutoki said.

1. Also known as Osaragi Nobutoki (1238–1323), the governor of Mutsu.
2. Hōjō Tokiyori. See above, sec. 184, n. 1.
3. The ordinary dress of samurai at the time.

216

The lay priest of Saimyōji, on a pilgrimage to the shrine of
Tsurugaoka, took the opportunity to visit the Lay Priest
Ashikaga Yoshiuji,[1] first sending a messenger ahead to an-
nounce his arrival. This is how he was entertained. With the
first round of drinks he was served dried abalone; with the
second, prawns; with the third, rice crackers. That was all.
Present on this occasion with the host were his wife and the
Abbot Ryūben.[2] After the entertainment, the lay priest of
Saimyōji said, "I've been waiting impatiently for that Ashi-
kaga dyed cloth you send me every year." Yoshiuji answered,

"I have some ready for you." He brought out thirty lengths of dyed cloth of different colors, and in Saimyōji's presence, had the cloth made up into short-sleeved kimonos by his waiting women. He sent them on afterwards.

This story was told by a man who witnessed the events and was still alive until recently.

1. The name is given in the text as Ashikaga Sama no Nyūdō, Sama being the chief of the bureau of horses, left division. Yoshiuji (1177–1242) was the son-in-law of Hōjō Yasutoki; his wife was thus an aunt of Tokiyori.
2. Ryūben (1206–83) was the Buddhist official (*bettō*) in charge of the temple at the Tsurugaoka Shrine.

217

A certain exceedingly rich man once said, "A man's first obligation is to devote himself with all his energies to making a fortune. It isn't worth living if you are poor. Only the rich man merits the name of 'man.' If you would like to make a fortune, the first thing you must do is to cultivate an appropriate frame of mind—a conviction that human life is eternal. You must never, even for a moment, consider it may be impermanent. This is the first caution. Next, you must remember never to satisfy your desires in anything. In this world, man has innumerable desires, both for himself and others. If he attempts to satisfy these desires, indulging his appetites, his money will not last long, even if he started with a million *zeni*.[1] Desires never cease, but there comes a time when your fortune is exhausted. It is quite impossible to satisfy unlimited desires with limited means. If desires germinate in your heart, you should dread them as an evil passion come to destroy you, and curb them severely. Do not gratify even small wants.

"Next, if you suppose that money may be used like a servant, you will never escape poverty. Money should be feared and dreaded like a master or god, not used as one pleases.

"Next, you must never be angry or resentful when faced by humiliation.

"Next, you must be honest and abide firmly by your promises.

"Riches will come to any man who obeys these rules as he seeks after profit, as surely as fire spreading to dry wood or water flowing downstream. When he has accumulated wealth so great it cannot be exhausted, his heart will be eternally at peace and happy, though he gives no thought to carousing and fleshly pleasures, though he refrains from decorating his house, and though he never fulfills his desires."

One might suppose that the reason for seeking wealth is so we may fulfill our desires, and the reason why money is precious is that it makes it possible to obtain what one wants. But if a man has desires and does not satisfy them, has money and does not use it, he is exactly the same as a poor man. What pleasure can he derive from it? The millionaire's prescriptions seem to urge men to forego their worldly desires and not grieve over poverty. But it is better not to have money than to hope for pleasure in satisfying a desire for wealth. For the man suffering from boils, the pleasure obtained by washing them is not as great as that of being freed from them altogether. At this point poverty and wealth lose all distinction. In the final stage, those at the highest level of enlightenment are the same as those at the lowest.[2] The man of powerful desires resembles one without desires.

1. A *zeni* was a copper coin. See above, sec. 60, n. 3.
2. Two of the six stages of thought regarding reality (*rokusokui*) recognized by Tendai Buddhists.

218

Foxes bite people. An equerry sleeping in the Horikawa palace had his leg bitten by a fox. Three foxes leapt on a junior priest one night as he was passing before the main building at the Ninnaji and bit him. He took out his knife to defend himself, and in the process ran two of the foxes through. One was stabbed to death, the other two escaped. The priest was bitten in many places, but nothing serious occurred.

219

The Shijō middle counselor[1] declared, "Tatsuaki[2] is a truly distinguished scholar of our art. The other day he came to me and said, 'I know it's a superficial thought, and extremely presumptuous of me to mention it, but I have wondered to myself if there were not something slightly peculiar about the fifth hole of the transverse flute. I mean, the *kan* hole is of the *hyō* tone,[3] and the fifth hole is of the *shimomu* tone. Between them is the *shōzetsu* tone. The *jō* hole is of the *sō* tone, and, next, the *saku* hole is of the *ōshiki* tone, with the *fushō* tone in between. Next, in the middle hole, is the *banshiki* tone, with the *rankei* tone in between. The *shinsen* tone is between the middle and sixth holes. In this manner, one semitone is omitted between each two holes, except for the fifth hole, which has no tone separating it from the *jō* hole.

The space between the two holes is, however, the same as for the others, and this causes the fifth hole to have an unpleasant sound. That is why the flutist always removes his mouth from the hole before blowing. Unless he does so, the sound will not harmonize with that of the other instruments. It is rare to find a man who blows this hole well.' His observation was most perceptive, and truly interesting. This was a case of 'pioneers fearing late-comers.' "

Some time later Kagemochi[4] commented, "The *shō*[5] is a tuned instrument, and you need only blow it. But with a flute, you must while blowing control the pitch with your breath. That is why a secret tradition exists relating to each hole. In addition, you must give each sound your own personality and spirit, and not only the fifth hole. It isn't enough to make it a rule not to blow directly into the fifth hole. If you play badly, the sound coming from any hole will be unpleasant. The skillful flutist will harmonize with the other instruments no matter which hole he blows. Any failure in harmonization of the melody is the fault of the player, and not a defect in the instrument."

1. Fujiwara no Takasuke (1293–1352), who became a middle counselor in 1330.
2. Toyohara Tatsuaki (1291?–1363?), a *gagaku* musician, was a renowned player of the *shō*, an instrument he taught the Emperor Go-Daigo.
3. The equivalents in tonic notes are: *kan*, E; *shōzetsu*, F; fifth (*go*), F sharp; *jō*, G; *saku*, A; *rankei*, A sharp; middle (*chū*), B; *shinsen*, C; sixth (*roku*), D.
4. Ōga Kagemochi (1292–1376) was a celebrated flutist.
5. The *shō* is sometimes called a "reed organ" in English; it consists of a cluster of small reed pipes.

I once ventured the opinion, "Everything in the provinces is coarse and ugly, except for *bugaku* at Ten'ōji,[1] which ranks with that in the capital." A musician from Ten'ōji replied, "The music at this temple is superior in that the instruments are tuned to standard pitch and the sounds blend better than elsewhere. This is because the standard pitches going back to the time of Prince Shōtoku are still preserved in the temple and used to guide us. I refer to the bell before what is popularly known as the Six Hours Hall.[2] The sound of this bell is precisely the tone of *ōshiki*.[3] The pitch naturally rises or falls according to the temperature. We therefore take as our standard pitch the sound during the period in the second month between the anniversary of the death of Buddha and that of the death of Prince Shōtoku. This is a secret tradition of our people. We use this sound to determine the value of all the others."

As a rule, the pitch of a bell should be the tone of *ōshiki*. This tone evokes an atmosphere of transience. It was the tone of the bells at the Monastery of Mutability at the Gion Shōja.[4] The bell for the Saionji was cast and recast again and again because they wished it to be in the *ōshiki* tone, but in vain. A bell was eventually found in a distant province. The sound of the bell of the Jōkongō-in[5] is also in the *ōshiki* tone.

1. More commonly called Tennōji, a large temple in Osaka, founded by Prince Shōtoku. Even today *bugaku* is performed there.
2. The Rokujidō was a hall where worship was carried out six times during the day. A bell sounded the times.
3. *Ōshiki* corresponds to the tonic note A. It is interesting that this tone was used in both East and West for tuning.
4. Gion Shōja is the Japanese name for the monastery in the Jetavana Grove where Shakyamuni Buddha taught. The bells at the Monastery

of Mutability (Mujō-in) sounded when a priest was dying. The celebrated opening lines of *Heike Monogatari* mention the "voices" of these bells.

5. A temple built by the Retired Emperor Go-Saga.

221

Old officers of the imperial police still tell today how "along about the Kenji and Kōan eras,[1] they used to make a funny-looking horse out of four or five lengths of dark-blue cloth as a decoration for the costume of the freed man[2] on the day of the Festival, using lampwicks for the tail and mane. They attached this horse to the man's jacket, which was painted with a spider-web design, and he went along singing the poem on the subject.[3] We always used to see him, and we thought he made a delightful sight."

In recent times the decorations have become more and more elaborate each year. So many kinds of heavy things are attached to the man's costume that his sleeves have to be held up by others, and the man himself, who does not even carry a spear, trudges along, breathing heavily, a most unappealing sight.

1. Kenji era, 1275–78; Kōan era, 1278–88. Both eras were during the reign of the Emperor Go-Uda.
2. The *hōben* seem to have been released criminals who served as guards at the lowest level of the imperial police (*kebiishi*).
3. Commentators refer to a poem of unknown origin: "Though a wild horse may be tied with a spider's web, you cannot trust a man who runs along two roads." The spider-web design on the jacket and the horse made of cloth allude to the poem.

222

When Jōgambō of Takedani[1] visited the Eastern Nijō palace, the former empress[2] asked him, "Which ceremony for the dead is the most efficacious?" He replied, "The *kōmyō shingon* and the *hōkyōin darani*."[3] Later, a disciple asked him, "Why did you say that? Why could you not say that nothing is superior to the *nembutsu?*" He replied, "I should gladly have said so, considering our sect, but I have never seen any sacred text which clearly states that saying the *nembutsu* at a memorial service is especially effective. I realized that I should be hard pressed for an answer if Her Majesty pursued the matter and asked what authority I had for recommending the *nembutsu*. I decided therefore to mention the *shingon* and *darani* for which unimpeachable authority exists."

1. Another name for Shūgen (1168–1251), a disciple of Hōnen and devout believer in the *nembutsu*. He lived as a hermit at Takedani, east of Kyoto.
2. Usually identified as Kinko (1232–1304), the consort of the Emperor Go-Fukakusa.
3. Two spells, used mainly by Shingon Buddhists, intended to free the dead from suffering and promote their enlightenment.

223

Tazu no Ōidono[1] had for his boyhood name Tazukimi. It is mistaken to suppose that he was given this name because he raised cranes.

1. Kujō Motoie (1203–80), one of the compilers of the anthology *Shoku-Kokinshū* (1265). *Tazu* means a crane; *ōidono* is a title designating a person in service at a provisional imperial palace.

224

The Lay Priest Arimune, the yin-yang diviner, came up to the capital from Kamakura and paid me a visit. As soon as he entered the house he reprimanded me. "Your garden is preposterously big. It's shocking, and quite unforgivable. An adept of the Way should exert himself to plant useful crops. You should leave only a single narrow path to your gate and cultivate the rest."

Truly, it is a wicked thing to allow the smallest parcel of land to lie idle. One should plant vegetables, medicinal herbs, and so on.

225

Ō no Hisasuke[1] relates that the Lay Priest Michinori[2] selected the most interesting dance steps and taught a woman called Iso no Zenji to perform them. She appeared in a white cloak with a dagger at her side and a man's hat on her head; that is why her dances were known as "men's dances." The daughter of this Zenji, a woman named Shizuka[3] followed her in this profession. This is the origin of the *shirabyōshi,* women performers who sang stories about the Buddhas and the gods. In later times Minamoto no Mitsuyuki[4] composed many pieces for them. There are also pieces written by the Emperor Go-Toba. It is said he taught them to Kamegiku.[5]

1. Ō no Hisasuke (1214–85), a court musician.
2. Fujiwara no Michinori (1106–59), a man of great learning, showed special interest in early Japanese entertainments. He took the Buddhist name of Shinzei.

3. Celebrated in many works as the mistress of Yoshitsune.
4. Minamoto no Mitsuyuki (1163–1244) was a poet and scholar of *Genji Monogatari*. He served the Retired Emperor Go-Toba.
5. A favorite *shirabyōshi* dancer of Go-Toba.

226

During the reign of the Emperor Go-Toba, a former official from Shinano named Yukinaga[1] enjoyed a reputation for learning. Once, when he was chosen to participate in a discussion on the *Yüeh-fu,*[2] he forgot two of the military virtues described in the poem *Dance of the Seven Virtues*. He accordingly acquired the nickname of Young Man of the Five Virtues. This nickname so distressed him that he abandoned scholarship and became a priest. The priest Jichin,[3] who made a practice of hiring men with artistic talent even as menials and treating them kindly employed this lay priest of Shinano.

Yukinaga wrote the *Heike Monogatari* and taught a blind man named Shōbutsu[4] to recite it. That is why the temple on the mountain[5] is described with special dignity. He wrote about Yoshitsune with a detailed knowledge, but omitted many facts about Noriyori,[6] perhaps because he did not know much about him. Shōbutsu, a native of the Eastern Provinces, questioned the soldiers from his part of the country about military matters and feats of arms, then got Yukinaga to write them down. *Biwa* entertainers[7] today imitate what was Shōbutsu's natural voice.

1. Yukinaga's name occurs in a few documents dated 1190–1202. The identification of Yukinaga as the author of *Heike Monogatari* is of great interest, but there is no supporting evidence.

2. A variety of Chinese poetry. Here, reference is probably being made to poems in this form by Po Chü-i, especially the *Dance of the Seven Virtues*.
3. Jichin Kashō was also known as Jien Sōjō. See above, sec. 67, n. 3.
4. Nothing is known about this man.
5. A reference to Enryakuji on Mount Hiei.
6. Minamoto no Noriyori (d. 1193), referred to here as Kaba no Kanja. He is not portrayed as an important character in *Heike Monogatari* even though he was a son of the famous Minamoto no Yoshitomo (1123–60).
7. *Biwa hōshi* were entertainers who dressed as priests. They recited *Heike Monogatari,* accompanying themselves on the *biwa.*

227

The *Six Daily Hours of Worship*[1] was compiled from various sacred books by a priest named Anraku,[2] a disciple of the High Priest Hōnen, for use in services. Later, a priest named Zenkambō from Uzumasa set it to music and put it in the form of a Buddhist hymn. This marked the beginning of the Single *Nembutsu*.[3] It began during the reign of the Emperor Go-Saga. The *Hymns on the Law* were also created by the same Zenkambō.

1. *Rokuji Raisan* were the texts used for the six-times-daily worship of Amida. See above, sec. 220, n. 2.
2. Anraku (d. 1207), a devoted propagandist of the Amidist faith, was put to death for transmitting these teachings to ladies of Go-Toba's court.
3. That is, one recitation of the *nembutsu* was enough to gain salvation. Earlier men had believed incessant repetitions were desirable.

228

The *nembutsu* ceremony at the Shaka Hall on Sembon Avenue was begun about the Bun'ei era by the High Priest Nyorin.[1]

1. Chōkū, a son of Fujiwara no Moroie. The Bun'ei era lasted from 1264 to 1275.

229

They say that a good carver uses a slightly dull knife. Myō-kan's[1] knife cut very poorly.

1. Identified by some scholars with a sculptor active in 780, but this is tentative.

230

They say there used to be a ghost in the Gojō Palace. The Fujiwara major counselor[1] related that once, when the courtiers were playing *go* in the Black Chamber, someone lifted the bamboo blinds and peeped in. "Who is it?" they cried and turned to look at it. A fox was squatting there, just like a man, watching them. At the shout of "It's a fox!" the creature became rattled and ran away. It must have been an inexperienced fox, a failure at working spells.

1. It is not clear if this refers to Fujiwara no Tameuji (1222–86) or Fujiwara no Tameyo (1250–1338), both distinguished poets.

231

The Sono chief of the imperial police and lay priest[1] was an incomparable cook. Once, when a magnificent carp had been offered to a certain household, everybody thought this would be a fine opportunity to see Sono display his skill at carving, but they hesitated, uncertain whether or not they dared propose this to him. But the chief, being the kind of man he was, said, "I have been carving a carp every day for the last one hundred days, I mustn't miss today. By all means let me have it." He proceeded to slice the carp. Everybody was amused, finding his response most appropriate to the occasion. But when a certain person told the Kitayama prime minister[2] what had happened, he said, "I find the story most contrived. How much better it would have been if he had said, 'If you have no one else to carve it, let me have the carp. I'll carve it.' Why should anyone have been slicing carp for a hundred days?" The man who told me the story said it had struck him as amusing, which it certainly was.

As a rule, it is preferable to act in a natural, unaffected manner, rather than achieve an amusing but contrived effect. It is excellent, when entertaining an unexpected guest for dinner, to act as if he had arrived most opportunely, but equally good to produce the dinner without making any special fuss. It shows true friendship to offer gifts even when there is no occasion, saying simply, "This is for you." It gives an unpleasant feeling if you act as if you are reluctant to part with the gift, in the hope that the recipient will appreciate it more, or if you pretend to be giving it as a forfeit for a bet you have lost.

1. Either Fujiwara no Motofuji (1276–1316) or Fujiwara no Motouji (1211–82).
2. Perhaps Saionji Sanekane (1249–1322), mentioned in sec. 118.

232

Men should be ignorant and without talent. A certain man had a son who was quite presentable in appearance, but when he engaged in conversation with people in his father's presence, he would quote passages from the *Book of History*. He sounded very learned, but he might better have refrained from such erudition before his seniors.

Again, a *biwa* had been brought to a certain man's house so that the assembled persons might hear a minstrel recite. It was noticed then that a fret was missing. The host commanded, "Somebody make another one and fix it to the instrument." One of the men present—a decent-looking person—said, "Have you an old ladle here? I'd like to use the handle." [1] I noticed then that he had long fingernails; obviously he played the *biwa*. But the *biwa,* when played by a blind minstrel, does not need anything so complicated. The man must have suggested the ladle to show off his knowledge of the art; it was embarrassing even as an outsider to listen to him. The handle of a ladle, as somebody pointed out, is not suitable as a fret for the *biwa* because it is made of inferior cypress wood.

The impression a young man creates—whether good or bad—is determined by even such trivial instances.

1. Commentators explain that the handle, being of dried-out cypress (*hinoki*), would be appropriate because the *biwa* is made of the same wood.

233

If you wish to avoid mistakes of any kind, there is no better way than to be sincere in whatever you do, respectful to every man without distinction, and scant of words.

Anybody—whether a man or woman, old or young—does well to maintain a purity of speech, but this quality in a young, handsome person produces an especially unforgettable, even seductive, appeal.

All mistakes originate with people's acting like experts thoroughly familiar with a subject, and looking down with an air of superiority on others.

234

If someone asks you a question you should never put him off with evasions, telling yourself, "I can't believe he doesn't know. I'd be a fool to give him a straightforward answer." Perhaps the man does know, but is asking in the hope of more precise information. Besides, can you be sure that not one person is really ignorant? It will sound sweeter-tempered if you answer him plainly.

How annoying it is for the other person if you write about something you know but he has not yet heard about, telling him merely, "I was shocked to learn about so and so." In this way you force him to send the return message, "What on earth has happened?" Even if the matter to which you allude has become common knowledge, some people naturally will have missed hearing it. You can hardly go wrong if you inform your correspondent what has happened in quite unambiguous terms.

Such lapses are typical of uncouth persons.

235

A man with no business will never intrude into an occupied house simply because he so pleases. If the house is vacant, on the other hand, travelers journeying along the road will enter with impunity, and even creatures like foxes and owls, undisturbed by any human presence, will take up their abodes, acting as if the place belonged to them. Tree spirits and other apparitions will also manifest themselves.

It is the same with mirrors: being without color or shape of their own, they reflect all manner of forms. If mirrors had color and shape of their own, they would probably not reflect other things.

Emptiness accommodates everything. I wonder if thoughts of all kinds intrude themselves at will on our minds because what we call our minds are vacant? If our minds were occupied, surely so many things would not enter them.

236

In Tamba there is a place called Izumo where they have built a splendid shrine in imitation of the Great Shrine.[1] This domain is ruled over by a certain Shida. One autumn he invited the holy man Shōkai and many other people to see him. "Come," he said, "let us worship at the Izumo Shrine. We'll have a feast of rice cakes too." He led them to the shrine, where they all worshiped and felt stirred by religious feeling. The stone lion and dog[2] before the shrine were set up back to back, facing away. This much impressed the holy man. "Ah, this is splendid!" he said in tears.

"These lions are placed most unusually. There must be a profound reason." He turned to the others. "Gentlemen, are you not filled with amazement by this extraordinary sight? How insensitive of you!" Each of them accordingly expressed his astonishment: "There is nothing like it elsewhere. We'll be sure to tell people when we return to the capital." The holy man, all the more fascinated, called to an elderly Shinto priest who looked knowledgeable and asked, "I am sure some tradition must account for the placing of the stone lions at this shrine. Would you kindly tell me a bit about it?" The priest answered, "The fact of the matter is, they were put that way by some mischievous boys. It's a disgrace." He went up to the lions, restored them to their normal position, and went away. The holy man's tears of emotion had been for nothing.

1. The Great Shrine of Izumo is on the Japan Sea, but the Izumo Shrine of this story was near Kyoto.
2. The *kara-shishi* (Chinese lion) and *koma-inu* (Korean dog) placed before Shinto shrines today are actually of stone and hardly to be moved by children, but those in Kenkō's day were probably made of wood.

237

I wonder if the placing of objects on a willow-work stand—whether lengthwise or sideways—depends on the object? Scrolls are placed lengthwise, parallel to the strips of willow, and are tied to the stand by passing a string of twisted paper through the spaces between the slats. Sanjō, the minister of the left, said, "It is good to place inkstones lengthwise too, because it keeps the brushes from rolling off." The calligraphers of the Kadenokōji school, however, never place their inkstones lengthwise, even casually. They always place the inkstone sideways on the stand.

Chikatomo,[1] the bodyguard of the retired emperor, wrote a document in seven articles which he called "Self-Praise." It is taken up entirely with trivial matters relating to horsemanship. Following this precedent, I have written my own seven articles of "self-praise."

1. Once when I went walking with a crowd of people, admiring the cherry blossoms, I saw near the Saishōkō-in a man galloping on a horse. I said, "If he gallops that horse once more the horse will collapse and he will fall off. Just keep watching for a while." The man raced the horse again as we stood there. When he stopped he pulled back the reins, only to overturn the horse and himself roll off into the mud. Everyone was impressed by the accuracy of my prediction.

2. When the present emperor[2] was still crown prince, he had his residence at the Madenokōji palace. Having business there, I visited the room where the Horikawa major counselor[3] was waiting in attendance. He had the fourth, fifth, and sixth scrolls of the *Analects* opened before him, and explained, "Just now His Highness wished to consult the passage where it says, 'I hate to see purple steal the glory from vermilion.'[4] He examined the text, but not finding the passage, commanded me to continue searching until I found it. I am still looking." I said, "You will find it at such and such a place in the ninth scroll." "That's wonderful," he said, and took the scroll to His Highness.

Such a display of knowledge would not be extraordinary even for a child, but people in the past used to praise themselves for the most trivial accomplishments. When the Emperor Go-Toba asked Lord Teika, "Is it bad to have two words for sleeve, *sode* and *tamoto,* in one poem?" Teika replied, "There is a poem, 'Are the flowering catkins the *tamoto* of the grasses in the autumn fields? When they come into ear they look like *sode* beckoning.'[5] In view of this precedent, what objection could there be?" Teika described the event pompously, "It was a providence bestowed by the Way of Poetry that I should have remembered the relevant poem in time. Truly I enjoyed great good fortune." The memorial on his achievements presented to the throne by His Excellency the Kujō Prime Minister Koremichi,[6] lists as matters for self-praise various unimpressive items.

3. The inscription on the bell at the Jōzaikō-in was drafted by Lord Arikane.[7] Yukifusa no Ason[8] wrote the fair copy, and when they were at last about to cast the bell, the lay priest in charge took out the rough draft and showed it to me. It contained the line, "Far beyond the blossoms, the voice of the bell, announcing evening, is heard one hundred *ri.*" I said, "I wonder if 'one hundred *ri*' is a mistake? The poem seems to be in the rhyme scheme of *yang-t'ang.*"[9] The priest said, "I am glad I showed it to you. This will redound to my credit." When he enquired of the author, the reply came from Arikane, "I made a mistake. You should change 'one hundred *ri*' to 'several *hang.*'" I wonder what "several *hang*" would mean. Several paces, perhaps? It is not clear.

4. Once, when I went on a pilgrimage to the Three Pagodas[10] in the company of a large party, I discovered inside the Jōgyō Hall at Yokawa an old plaque bearing the words Ryūge-in. A priest at the temple explained officiously, "Scholars have long attempted unsuccessfully to determine whether the plaque was written by Sari or Kōzei."[11] I said, "If it is by Kōzei, it should be signed on the back. If it is by Sari, it will not be signed." The back was covered with dust and

filthy with cobwebs, but when it was carefully cleaned and wiped, we could all see Kōzei's title, name, and the date, clearly inscribed. Everybody was impressed.

5. When the holy man Dōgen[12] preached at the Naranda Temple, he forgot what the Eight Disasters were. He asked, "Does anyone remember?", but his pupils had all forgotten. At this point I spoke up from the congregation and asked, "I wonder if they might be such and such?" at which everyone marveled.

6. Once, in the company of the Abbot Kenjo,[13] I witnessed the incantation over the perfumed water.[14] The abbot left before the ceremony was over, but could not find his attendant priest when he got outside the entrance. He sent some other priests back into the hall to look for him, but after a long wait they reappeared only to say, "There were so many people all dressed alike that we couldn't find him." Thereupon the abbot said to me, "How provoking! You go and look for him." I went back inside and came out with the man immediately.

7. On the fifteenth day of the second month, a night of bright moonlight, I went late to worship at the temple in Sembon, and was listening to the ceremony, having entered by the back door alone and heavily shading my face, when a beautiful woman of unusually distinguished appearance made her way into the assemblage and sat down leaning against my knee, so close that I thought her perfume would be transferred to my robe. This would have been embarrassing, so I slipped unobtrusively to the side, only for her to edge up against me again as before. I finally got up. Later, an old gentlewoman, in service with a certain noble family, said to me in the course of her gossip about various unimportant matters, "Something happened that made me look

down on you for being a terrible stick. There's someone who is still annoyed with you for your coldness." I said, "I haven't the least idea what you are talking about," and let the matter drop.

I subsequently learned that on the night of the ceremony a certain person sitting in the special section of the temple reserved for the nobility noticed me in the congregation and, dressing up a waiting woman suitably, sent her to me with the directions, "Speak to him if things seem to be going well, and when you get back tell us what he does in return. This ought to be amusing." A trick had been played on me.

1. Nakahara Chikatomo served under the Emperors Horikawa and Toba.
2. The Emperor Go-Daigo ascended the throne in 1318. In 1331 he was exiled to Oki and a prince was enthroned as Kōgon. Go-Daigo was crown prince between 1308 and 1318.
3. Possibly Fujiwara no Moronobu (1274–1321).
4. From *Analects* XVII, 18. In Waley's translation: "The Master said, 'I hate to see roan killing red, I hate to see the tunes of Chêng corrupting Court music, I hate to see sharp mouths overturning kingdoms and clans.' "
5. The poem is *Kokinshū* 243, by Ariwara no Muneyana. The words *sode* and *tamoto* both mean "sleeve," but *tamoto* designates the hanging part.
6. Fujiwara no Koremichi (1093–1165), mentioned above in sec. 6.
7. Sugawara no Arikane (1249–1321), a distinguished scholar.
8. Fujiwara no Yukifusa (d. 1337) joined the Emperor Go-Daigo in his flight from Kyoto in 1331. The events described must antedate that year.
9. The poem on the bell, in Chinese, should have rhymed throughout in *-ang,* but one line mistakenly ended in *-i.*
10. The three pagodas on Mount Hiei.
11. Fujiwara no Sari (944–998), a noted calligrapher. For Kōzei see above, sec. 25, n. 10.
12. See above, sec. 179.
13. Kenjo Sōjō (1295–1330) was the son of Fujiwara no Kimmori (1249–1317).

14. The ceremony, known as *kaji kōzui,* was performed at the Shingon-in on the twelfth, thirteenth, and fourteenth days of the first month.

239

The fifteenth day of the eighth month and the thirteenth day of the ninth month are governed by the constellation Lou.[1] This constellation being a particularly bright one, these are good nights for enjoying the moon.

1. One of the twenty-eight "celestial mansions" distinguished by the Chinese yin-yang practitioners.

240

Deep indeed is the love of a man who valiantly persists in his courtship though "the observant eyes of the fisherwomen on the strand of Shinobu are bothersome," and "even in the darkness of Kurabu Mountain the watchers are many." [1] Such an affair will surely leave the girl with many unforgettable memories. But if her parents and brothers permit the courtship and are only too glad to welcome the young man[2] into the family, it is most disappointing. If a woman, hard pressed financially, announces her intention of marrying any man with money who will have her,[3] even an old priest twice her age, or a crude easterner, a go-between will soon be describing the match to both parties in most attractive terms, and some man will eventually marry a woman who is no less a stranger to him than he is to her. What a sad state of affairs! What can they possibly have to talk about? There would be an inexhaustible fund of stories to draw on if they could recollect the years and months of hardship before they came together or the difficulties encountered in the path of love.

As a rule, marriages arranged by another person are likely to involve many disagreeable things. Even if a woman is beautiful[4] and her husband of low birth, ugly, and old, he may well look down on her, thinking, "Would any woman be likely to throw her life away on a wretch like me?" He himself, when confronted by his new wife, will feel embarrassed about his appearance, making things all the worse.

The man who has never hesitated under a cloudy moon on a night fragrant with plum blossoms, or has no memories of the dawn moon in the sky as he started to walk through the dewy gardens inside the palace gate, had better have nothing to do with love.

1. The two parts of the poems quoted here are hackneyed in their imagery, but their exact source is unknown.
2. The wording is so vague that we cannot be sure who welcomes whom. Some commentators think that the boy's parents and brothers welcome the girl.
3. Literally, "if there is water which invites" (*sasou mizu araba*), an allusion to the famous poem by Ono no Komachi: "So lonely am I, a floating weed severed at the roots, were there water to invite me, I should follow it, I think." The meaning here is that the woman will go with any man who asks her.
4. The words *yoki onna* can mean either "a beautiful woman" or "a woman of good birth."

241

The full moon does not keep its roundness even a little while; it at once begins to wane. The man indifferent to such things may not see much change in the course of a single night. The worsening of an illness too does not pause in its headlong course, until the hour of death approaches. However, as long as a man's illness is not so critical that he is actually confronted by death, he grows accustomed to the idea that life will go on much the same forever, and only after he has accomplished many things in this life will he turn to quiet practice of the Way. But when a man is suddenly taken ill and faced by death, he realizes he has accomplished not one of his plans. He helplessly regrets the years and months of laziness, and resolves that if he should recover this time and live out his full life, he will unflaggingly strive days and nights on end to accomplish this or that. The sickness in the meanwhile grows steadily worse, until he loses consciousness and, in a state of violent agitation, breathes his last. This is true of the vast majority of people. Everyone should waste no time in taking this to heart.

If you imagine that once you have accomplished your ambitions you will have time to turn to the Way, you will discover that your ambitions never come to an end. In our dreamlike existence, what is there for us to accomplish? All ambitions are vain delusions. You should realize that, if desires form in your heart, false delusions are leading you astray; you should do nothing to fulfill them. Only when you abandon everything without hesitation and turn to the Way will your mind and body, unhindered and unagitated, enjoy lasting peace.

242

Man is eternally swayed by the pleasing or displeasing circumstances around him, thanks to his constant preoccupation with pleasure and pain. Pleasure is liking and loving. We never cease our pursuit of this happiness. The pleasure we desire first of all is that of fame. There are two kinds of fame: glory derived from one's conduct, or from one's talents. The next pleasure desired is that of lust, the third of appetite. None of man's other desires can equal these three. They arise from a perverted view of life, and cause innumerable griefs. It is best not to seek them.

243

When I turned eight years old I asked my father, "What sort of thing is a Buddha?" My father said, "A Buddha is what a man becomes." I asked then, "How does a man become a Buddha?" My father replied, "By following the teachings of Buddha." "Then, who taught the Buddha to teach?" He again replied, "He followed the teachings of the Buddha before him." I asked again, "What kind of Buddha was the first Buddha who began to teach?" At this my father laughed and answered, "I suppose he fell from the sky or else he sprang up out of the earth."

My father told other people, "He drove me into a corner, and I was stuck for an answer." But he was amused.

SELECTED BIBLIOGRAPHY

Of the numerous editions of *Tsurezuregusa* I have found the following most helpful.

Matsuo Satoshi. *Tsurezuregusa Zenshaku.* Tokyo, Shimizu Shoin, 1957.

Nishio Minoru. *Hōjōki, Tsurezuregusa,* in *Nihon Bungaku Taikei.* Tokyo, Iwanami Shoten, 1957.

Sano Yasutarō. *Tsurezuregusa Shinkō.* Revised edition. Tokyo, Fukumura Shoten, 1947.

Tachibana Jun'ichi. *Tsurezuregusa.* Tokyo, Musashino Shoin, 1949.

Tanabe Tsukasa. *Tsurezuregusa Shochū Shūsei.* Tokyo, Yūbun Shoin, 1962.

Tomikura Jirō. *Kenkō Hōshi Kenkyū.* Tokyo, Tōyōkaku, 1937.

INDEX

Abe no Yoshihira, 142
Accomplishments, 69, 104–5, 134–35, 144
Action, 162
Adachi Yasumori, 158
Adachi Yoshikage, 157–58
Adashino, 7, 8n
Agrimony (fujibakama), 123, 126n
Akikane, 171
Ambition, 143–44, 160–62, 200
Amida Buddha, 36; statues of, 26, 27n
Amidabutsu (priest), 75–76
Analects, quoted, 66n, 73n, 105n, 109nn, 162n, 194, 196n
Animals, 101–4, 107–8, 157
Anki, Retired Empress (Fujiwara Yūshi), 90–91n
Anraku, 187
Antiquity, charms of, 23–24; see also Customs; Language
Antlers, of deer, 134
Archery, 78, 104
Architecture, 10, 32–33, 50–51, 71
Arimune, 185
Ariwara no Muneyana, quoted, 195
Ariwara no Narihira, 60, 60n
Arrogance, 113–15
Arrowroot vine, 59, 126
Arts, 104–5, 134–35, 144–45, 159; see also Accomplishments; Expertise
Ashi (aji), 130
Ashikaga Yoshiuji, 178
Asters, 123
Asuka River, 25, 26n
Atsushige, 114–15
Autumn, 18–20 passim
Ayanokōji, Prince (Shōe), 10, 11n

Ballads, 13–16
Bamboo, 169
Beans and bean husks, 62
Beauty: of man, 4; of woman, 9; of surroundings, 10; of sky, 22
Beginning, and end, 115–22; see also Impermanence
Behavior, 81; unsuitable, 94–95, 112–13; natural, 189
Bellflowers, 123
Bells, 182; inscription, 195
Ben no Menoto, quoted, 122
Birds, 10–11, 19, 101–4, 107–8, 142, 173–74
Biwa, 17, 62–63, 186, 190
Black Chamber, 153
Boastfulness, 113–15
Bommō-kyō, cited, 152
Bon Festival, 21n
Books and reading, 12
Boxes, attachment of cords to, 80
Buddha, 182, 201; teaching on liquor, 152; see also Amida Buddha
Buddhism, influence on Kenkō's work, xiv, xvii–xviii
Bugaku, 182
Burnet, 123

Caps, court, 58
Carp, 100, 188–89
Carriages, 58; art of driving, 95
Caution, 158–59
Ceremonies, 19–21 passim, 196; of abdication, 28; see also Customs
Ceremony (term), 145
Chang-an, 67n
Change, 66, 71, 77, 137–38; useless, 167; see also Beginning and end; Impermanence
Chao Ming, Prince, 12

[205]

[211]